The American History Series

SERIES EDITORS

John Hope Franklin, *Duke University*

Abraham S. Eisenstadt, *Brooklyn College*

Arthur S. Link
Princeton University
GENERAL EDITOR FOR HISTORY

Gary W. Reichard
THE UNIVERSITY OF MARYLAND

Politics as Usual

The Age of Truman and Eisenhower

HARLAN DAVIDSON, INC.
ARLINGTON HEIGHTS, ILLINOIS 60004

Library of Congress Cataloging-in-Publication Data

Reichard, Gary W., 1943–
    Politics as usual : the age of Truman and Eisenhower / Gary W. Reichard.
        p.   cm. — (American history series)
    Bibliography: p.
    Includes index.
    ISBN 0-88295-856-9
    1. United States—Politics and government—1945–1953. 2. United States—Politics and government—1953–1961. 3. Truman, Harry S., 1884–1972. 4. Eisenhower, Dwight D. (Dwight David), 1890–1969.
I. Title. II. Series: American history series (Arlington Heights, Ill.)
E813.R36   1988   87-20726
973.918—dc19   CIP

Manufactured in the United States of America
92 91 90 89 88 1 2 3 4 5 6 7 LP

To Jen and Jamie

FOREWORD

Every generation writes its own history, for the reason that it sees the past in the foreshortened perspective of its own experience. This has certainly been true of the writing of American history. The practical aim of our historiography is to offer us a more certain sense of where we are going by helping us understand the road we took in getting where we are. If the substance and nature of our historical writing is changing, it is precisely because our own generation is redefining its direction, much as the generation that preceded us redefined theirs. We are seeking a newer direction, because we are facing new problems, changing our values and premises, and shaping new institutions to meet new needs. Thus, the vitality of the present inspires the vitality of our writing about our past. Today's scholars are hard at work reconsidering every major field of our history: its politics, diplomacy, economy, society, mores, values, sexuality, and status, ethnic, and race relations. No less significantly, our scholars are using newer modes of investigation to probe the ever-expanding domain of the American past.

Our aim, in this American History Series, is to offer the reader a survey of what scholars are saying about the central themes and issues of American history. To present these themes and issues, we have invited scholars who have made notable contributions to the respective fields in which they are writing.

Each volume offers the reader a sufficient factual and narrative account for perceiving the larger dimensions of its particular subject. Addressing their respective themes, our authors have undertaken, moreover, to present the conclusions derived by the principal writers on these themes. Beyond that, the authors present their own conclusions about those aspects of their respective subjects that have been matters of difference and controversy. In effect, they have written not only about where the subject stands in today's historiography but also about where they stand on their subject. Each volume closes with an extensive critical essay on the writings of the major authorities on its particular theme.

The books in this series are designed for use in both basic and advanced courses in American history. Such a series has a particular utility in times such as these, when the traditional format of our American history courses is being altered to accommodate a greater diversity of texts and reading materials. The series offers a number of distinct advantages. It extends and deepens the dimensions of course work in American history. In proceeding beyond the confines of the traditional textbook, it makes clear that the study of our past is, more than the student might otherwise infer, at once complex, sophisticated, and profound. It presents American history as a subject of continuing vitality and fresh investigation. The work of experts in their respective fields, it opens up to the student the rich findings of historical inquiry. It invites the student to join, in major fields of research, the many groups of scholars who are pondering anew the central themes and problems of our past. It challenges the student to participate actively in exploring American history and to collaborate in the creative and rigorous adventure of seeking out its wider reaches.

John Hope Franklin
Abraham S. Eisenstadt

ACKNOWLEDGMENTS

This book is based largely on the works of other scholars who have written on the years of the Truman and Eisenhower presidencies, but it is also grounded in my research at both the Truman and Eisenhower Libraries. For generous assistance in support of that research, I wish to express appreciation to the Graduate School and the College of Humanities of the Ohio State University, and to the Harry S. Truman Library Institute. A Moody Research Grant from the Lyndon Baines Johnson Foundation and a grant from the Everett M. Dirksen Congressional Leadership Research Center also provided support for some of the research underlying this volume.

While conceding that responsibilities for any errors or shortcomings that remain must inevitably be mine, I wish to thank, for their helpful suggestions, my colleague Keith W. Olson, the two scholars who read and criticized an early version for Harlan Davidson, and, of course, the editors of this series, Abraham Eisenstadt and John Hope Franklin. For her good-natured and highly professional clerical assistance through successive drafts of the manuscript, I owe thanks to Vonda J. Harper. Finally, I am especially grateful to Eric M. Schwier, whose steady encouragement along the way was very important to my completing this project.

To my children Jennifer and Jamie—products of a later era—I dedicate this book, with love.

Gary W. Reichard
College Park, Maryland

CONTENTS

PREFACE

Historians constantly struggle with the problem of periodization, and historians of the most recent past confront the toughest problem of all. Without benefit of hindsight normally available to students of the past, it is difficult to sort the years into "eras" with any degree of confidence.

Not long ago, the term "postwar America" was unambiguous, synonymous with "the United States since 1945." In most American colleges and universities, this period was treated inadequately by the survey course, if at all. If covered, the era was viewed as an entity, dominated by the Cold War, the baby boom, suburbia, and a loosely defined "post–New Deal" political consensus.

As the end of the twentieth century nears, such an approach to the study of half of the century begs important questions. How can the teacher—or student—of history claim any degree of analytic understanding while lumping together as "postwar America" such disparate events as summitry, the Little Rock school desegregation crisis, voters' eight-year-long love affair with Dwight Eisenhower, the anti-Vietnam War protests, détente, Watergate, the frustrations of the Carter presidency, and the "Reagan revolution"? If periodization is justifiable at all in the study of history, then surely the time has arrived to attempt some sensible division of the nation's recent past.

Even in the case of time periods in the more distant past, particular decisions on periodization are open to question and criticism. The "middle period," for example—that amorphous era between the founding of the Republic and the coming of the Civil War—has been divided up in numerous ways by contending schools of historians. So it is likely to be with attempts to set apart "eras" in the recent period. But it will not advance our understanding of that period if we avoid the challenge.

This book takes the perspective that the decade and a half following World War II constitutes a discrete and identifiable historical era in recent American history, at least insofar as politics is concerned. True, the issues and forces influencing political life during these years were diverse: an ever-present Cold War, a full-blown civil rights "issue," the challenge posed by rapidly developing young nations, and a seemingly boundless national economic growth accompanied by dramatic technological changes. But it is equally true that these elements were a *continuous* political presence throughout the period. Moreover, American politics in these years reflected—if not exactly harmony—a seemingly purposeful equilibrium. Though anti-Communist hysteria for a time disturbed the calm, the years of the Truman and Eisenhower presidencies were not generally marked by the bitter partisan divisiveness of either the New Deal years or the superheated 1960s. As studies showed, voters in the postwar years were generally satisfied with the choices afforded by the two major parties and with the system as it was.

The two presidents who led the nation in these years, Harry S. Truman and Dwight D. Eisenhower, faced a common problem. In the years after World War II, the American electorate seemed intent on creating political deadlock. Nominally there existed a firm Democratic majority, yet for more than half of the fifteen-year period, the White House and Capitol Hill were controlled by opposing parties. For most of the remaining time, the Democrats controlled both branches, but only in theory. This situation particularly affected domestic politics. Truman's plans for domestic reform were stalemated by a "conservative coalition" of Republicans and southern Democrats who assumed the role of a political opposition, and Eisenhower, despite his remarkable hold on popular affections, seemed steadily to lose influence with the Democratic-controlled Congress after 1954.

The political deadlock that prevailed in these years, based as it was on the apparent general satisfaction of the public, has been viewed variously as equilibrium, stability, frustration, and stagnation. But, however it is portrayed, the period served as a staging ground for the bursts of energy and national crises that followed in an almost inevitable countercycle. In the context of the dramatic, near-cataclysmic events both preceding and following, the years 1945–1960 can best be understood as the last sustained period when "politics as usual" prevailed in the United States.

CHAPTER ONE

Truman's Trial Period, 1945-1948

To many Americans, it must have seemed that Franklin D. Roosevelt would be president forever. Several million voters had never voted for anyone else at the top of the ticket; many more millions had never experienced any other leader in the White House. Thus news of FDR's death in April 1945—despite the fact that rumors of his ill health had circulated for weeks—was greeted with disbelief and unacceptance. "It doesn't seem possible," remarked a Detroit woman. "It seems to me that he will be back on the radio tomorrow reassuring us all that it was just a mistake."

Roosevelt's passing gave new significance to the dramatic events that had marked the Democratic convention the previous summer. After much backroom maneuvering, the party had substituted Senator Harry S. Truman of Missouri on the national ticket for then-Vice President Henry Wallace. A loyal New Deal supporter in his second term in the Senate, Truman had received considerable (and favorable) press coverage for chairing the Senate Committee to Investigate the National Defense Program in the early 1940s. His selection had dashed the vice presidential hopes of the southern favorite, James S. Byrnes, as well as turned Wallace out. Even at the time, speculation arose that, as *Time* noted, the outcome "had more than Throttlebottom proportions ... [as] each delegate kept uppermost in mind that his choice for Vice President might become President."

Truman's nomination reflected the combined efforts of powerful labor leaders and big-city bosses. Known as a strong New Dealer, internationalist, party loyalist, and moderate on race questions, and hailing from a border state, Truman clearly qualified as a unity candidate. The press quickly dubbed the nomination "the second Missouri Compromise." Yet because Truman had replaced the liberal Wallace, his nomination was widely regarded as a setback for the forces of progressivism.

New President, New Problems

Harry Truman had little time to clarify public impressions of him before taking the oath of presidential office a little after 7:00 PM on April 12, 1945. To most he remained an unknown political quantity. Predictably, however, the public rallied to the new leader in the aftermath of Roosevelt's death. The spirit of cooperation was especially noticeable in Congress, where Truman had been a well-liked and respected member of the club. Above all, he was viewed as safe—and probably at least competent, even if not possessing the stuff of greatness. "Truman is honest and patriotic and has a head full of good horse sense," wrote former Vice President John Garner to House Speaker Sam Rayburn. "Besides, he [has] guts. All of this can be made into a good President." And the new chief executive seemed to have one quality FDR had lacked: "To Harry Truman," noted a news periodical, "a promise is a promise, something to be kept."

At first, absorbed in the final stages of World War II, Truman could give little attention to domestic matters. He tried to reassure progressive elements in the party, however, by announcing his intent to carry on Roosevelt's policies and to stand by the 1944 Democratic platform, the most liberal program on which FDR had ever run. Then, after the end of the war in Europe and Asia, in his first major address on domestic policy (September 6), Truman called for enactment of a far-reaching reform program. Among the twenty-one points he urged were Social Security extension, housing legislation, national health insurance, an increased minimum wage, further regional development programs modeled on the Tennessee Valley Authority (TVA), a full employment bill, and continuation of wartime wage and price controls. Some of his proposals related directly to the task of reconversion from war; others he could not expect to get right away. But Truman had set his agenda. The proposals of September 1945, which political commentators later labeled the "Fair Deal," reflected Truman's Senate record. They also raised the hackles of conservatives. "Now, nobody should have any doubt," remarked House Minority Leader Joseph Martin. "Not even President Roosevelt ever asked so much at one sitting. It is just a case of out–New Dealing the New Deal."

By late 1945, neither Truman nor Congress had done much planning for demobilization or economic reconversion. Both processes, consequently, were marked by disorganization that sometimes approached chaos. Demobilization—the mustering out of millions of American servicemen—occurred much faster than Truman wanted, and he acted powerless to stop it. Strong pressures existed: mothers, sweethearts, wives, and sisters staged noisy protest rallies at home, and thousands of servicemen demonstrated in Germany and the Philippines against the administration's initial plans for gradual demobilization. Though the president feared the results of an unregulated infusion of veterans back into the economy, and worried that postwar tensions required maintaining a credible U.S. military force, he capitulated. By early 1945, demobilization had become "disintegration" (in Truman's later phrase), despite the administration's attempt to implement a graduated "point system" to phase soldiers out of uniform. From a peak of 12 million in 1945, the American armed services shrank to 3 million a year later, and declined by another 50 percent by mid-1948.

The confusion accompanying the demobilization was not really Truman's fault; probably no president could have altered its chaotic course. Responsibility lay with the American public, which proved too impatient to accept the reasonable, phased process the administration had designed. Still, the president's image was tarnished by his apparent irresolution during the episode.

Truman also gave the impression of weakness in his reaction to issues related to economic reconversion. He appeared to vacillate in handling unemployment, price and wage problems, and labor-management strife, thereby confusing other politicians and the public. By late 1945, the succession of stormy events surrounding reconversion left the president in a difficult political position. The Gallup poll showed a decline in public support, from 82 percent in November 1945 to 45 percent by July 1946, and then to 32 percent three months later.

Congress, nominally Democratic but controlled by a "conservative coalition" of Republicans and anti–New Deal (mostly southern) Democrats, was no help in keeping reconversion systematic. A planned program for economic retooling would have required far more government regimentation than controlling congressional forces were willing to tolerate. Roosevelt's National Resources Planning Board had already been voted out of existence by 1945. The fact that Truman's cabinet and a number of key agencies experienced considerable turnover in personnel also hampered reconversion efforts.

Returning veterans received some direct help, as a result of the 1944 Servicemen's Readjustment Act, popularly known as the GI Bill. In addition to granting mustering-out pay and a maximum of fifty-two weeks of unemployment compensation, the GI Bill also provided for an employment service, educational benefits, business loans, and home and farm loan guarantees. The measure greatly assisted in economic reconversion, and provided needed financial and psychological security to individual veterans. Within ten years, about 7.8 million veterans—just over half of those eligible—used the GI Bill's education benefits, while nearly 3.8 million took advantage of the loan guarantees. At an estimated cost of over $20 billion in those ten years, the GI program proved a bargain to American society. It also kept Harry Truman's political stock from falling out of sight in the first year of his presidency.

Truman's problems were bad enough, however. Organized labor and its champions in Congress insisted that wages, kept down by wartime controls, now be allowed to rise at least as rapidly as prices. Unions also wanted to reverse policies they saw as discriminatory against workers, symbolized by the wartime Smith–Connally War Labor Disputes Act; specifically, they sought federal guarantees for the right of collective bargaining, including protection of the union shop and closed shop. Business interests, on the other hand, and conservatives (including both southern Democrats and Republicans, for slightly different reasons), perceived such demands as radical and dangerous to the economy. Bereft of an effective planning agency and personally inexperienced in exercising his powers, the president faced an apparent no-win situation.

Truman's reactions in the circumstances were neither consistent nor successful, and he managed to satisfy no one. The problems of wages and prices, of course, were directly interrelated. The leading public fear after the war was that depression and widespread unemployment would return; in fall 1945, 42 percent of Americans singled out "jobs" as the nation's foremost problem. But Truman was more concerned about the possibility of galloping inflation and a consequent worsening of labor-management conflict over wages. He believed, therefore, that price ceilings and allocation quotas had to be retained. In his State of the Union address in January 1945, he proposed extending the authority of the Office of Price Administration (OPA) beyond its scheduled termination date of June 30, 1946. "Inflationary pressures," Truman warned the public in a nationally broadcast speech, could produce "an inflation and a crash ... much more serious than 1920."

Polls showed that most American favored retention of controls in early 1946, but the president ran into strong congressional opposition. Many conservatives had favored killing off OPA in 1945, their sentiments captured in Republican Clare Hoffman's bitter comment that he was "sick and tired of OPA." Once the war was over, Ohio Senator Robert A. Taft, a leading contender for the Republican nomination in 1948, took a prominent part in the attack on controls. In fact, Taft's zeal on the issue may have ultimately helped to deny him the nomination, making him seem a more extreme conservative than he was. "Few issues of his long career," wrote Taft's biographer James Patterson in *Mister Republican,* "did more to stamp him in the eyes of his critics as a friend of business and an enemy of the poor man."

Confronted by this opposition and by dissension within the cabinet, Truman lessened his chances for success in the struggle by permitting piecemeal erosion of controls, both in response to lobbying by industry and in order to obtain strike-ending wage settlements in major industries, such as steel. In June, he won extension of OPA in the Price Control Act of 1946, but anticontrol amendments so hobbled the measure that it was no victory. In response to this emasculation of the Act, the liberal Chester Bowles resigned as director of economic stabilization and Truman vetoed it, stunning proadministration Democrats, who had supported the measure in the belief that it was the best that could be passed. When prices rose sharply, the public was furious with Truman. Three weeks later, the president lamely accepted a slightly different extension bill. There is no question that the OPA fight cost Truman dearly, particularly with liberals, who had distrusted him since 1944 for replacing Henry Wallace.

Similar problems marked other reconversion episodes. The proposed Full Employment Act, a major part of the domestic program Truman announced in fall 1945, was a case in point. The final product contrasted sharply with the bill's original Keynesian objectives. Proposed by liberal stalwarts in the Senate, such as James Murray of Montana and Robert F. Wagner of New York, the measure initially sought to establish a full-employment national budget, with machinery to determine the degree of federal activity needed to sustain full employment and to ensure such intervention. As signed into law in February 1946, the measure bore the significantly shortened title, "Employment Act," and the federal commitment was scaled down from full to "maximum" employment, as government intervention was made discretionary rather than mandatory. The final bill was not much of a victory for Truman, even if the Council of Economic Advisors it established proved a permanent benefit. Yet it would not be fair to say that the compromise resulted from lack of will on Truman's part. In the political climate of early 1946, marked by fears of inflation and impatience with big government, he could not have gotten much more from Congress, no matter what he had done.

In the first year after the war, the administration had its hands full with an endless string of strikes affecting nearly all major industries. In these matters, too, Truman frequently seemed incompetent, intemperate, or both. In certain critical sectors of the economy, the administration responded by taking over whole industries; this occurred in the first major postwar work stoppage, the oil industry (September 1945), and on eight other occasions before June 1946. But the president also tried to be conciliatory, appealing to labor and management to cooperate with one another. A White House–initiated conference of labor and management representatives held in November 1945 failed to produce any solutions, though it got the two sides talking.

The number of strikes increased sharply during the winter of 1945–1946. In February alone, 23 million worker-days were lost due to stoppages, and at one time or other during the spring virtually every major industry was crippled. The main issue was almost always wages. Faced with higher prices, workers resented loss of overtime—a reduction of about 30 percent in their take-home pay.

The strikes evoked a strong reaction. The National Association of Manufacturers led the antilabor forces, whipping up public hostility to unions. But consumers may not have needed much encouragement. A Gallup poll in October 1945—before the strikes had become widespread—showed a 74 percent positive response to the question of whether the government should take a strong stand against unions during the reconversion period. Nor was antilabor sentiment confined to Republicans. In the Seventy-ninth Congress (1945–1946), Democrats sponsored one-fifth of the bills introduced to regulate unions. Southern Democrats viewed the "radicalism" of organized labor with special hostility.

Truman recognized the strength of antilabor sentiments, though he appreciated that organized labor had contributed significantly to the Democratic vote (and treasury) since 1936. In December 1945 he called for strong new labor legislation, including two important features: fact-finding boards to recommend settlements in cases of dispute, and "cooling-off" periods to delay work stoppages while such investigations were being conducted. Liberal supporters of labor objected less to these relatively moderate proposals than to Truman's handling of the postwar strikes. In their eyes, the president's reluctance to confront corporate leadership, like his conduct in the struggles over price controls and full employment, signaled a lack of resolve and inadequate leadership.

The strikes of early 1946 involved the most basic and important economic issues. The conflict in the steel industry was typical. Management balked at an 18½-cent-per-hour wage increase recommended by a government fact-finding board, but not because of the amount of the proposed hike. Rather, management wanted to force the government to yield on price levels and allow prices to match any wage boost. In this instance, management won, and prices were permitted to rise to provide for the disputed wage increase. This undermined the authority of the beleaguered OPA, thus heightening the concerns of liberals who favored price controls.

Stoppages in the coal and railroad industries also had broad ramifications. The coal strike, called by intransigent United Mine Workers (UMW) leader John L. Lewis for April 1, 1946, idled some 400,000 soft-coal miners and quickly slowed the steel, auto, and railroad industries. After the mine workers rejected the recommendations of government fact finders, President Truman ordered government seizure of the coal mines in May. From this point forward bitter enmity existed between Truman and Lewis. To the president, Lewis seemed "a Hitler at heart, a demagogue in action, and a traitor in fact."

The situation quickly worsened. With the coal mines under federal control and the outlook shaky for the miners' contract, two major railroad unions—the Brotherhood of Locomotive Engineers and the Brotherhood of Railroad Trainmen—voted to reject a government-proposed wage settlement as inadequate, setting May 18 as the date for a shutdown of the railroads. Truman secured a five-day delay of the strike, but on May 22 the two railway unions turned down a second, more generous, recommendation by the president. On the next day the railroads stopped running.

Truman could take no more. On May 24 he went before Congress to ask for legislation authorizing the drafting of workers who struck vital industries. An original draft version of the speech, no doubt never intended for delivery, fully captured the president's deep anger and frustration:

> ... I am tired of government's being flouted, vilified[,] and now I want you men who are my comrades in arms[,] you men who fought the battles to save the nation just as I did twenty-five years ago[,] to come along with me and eliminate the Lewises, the Whitneys[,] the Johnstons, the Communist Bridges[,] and the Russian Senators and Representatives and really make this a government of[,] by[,] and for the people. . . .
>
> Let's give the country back to the people. Let's put transportation and production back to work, hang a few traitors[,] make our country safe for democracy[,] tell Russia where to get off[,] and make the United Nations work. . . .

Even the sanitized speech Truman delivered caused consternation in Congress—not only among Democrats friendly to labor, but among conservative Republicans who considered it too drastic. It was Senator Taft, in fact, who was primarily responsible for defeating the president's harsh proposal for a worker draft, which for a time seemed likely to pass despite a last-minute settlement of the rail strike that had been negotiated by White House aide John Steelman.

Truman's estrangement from labor seemed beyond repair, carrying ominous implications for his political future. In June, however, he surprised friend and foe alike by vetoing the Case bill, a measure that proposed a number of limitations on union practices. Truman's motives and actions during the period of labor crises in 1946 invite conjecture. Essentially, his decision to veto the Case bill seems consistent with his underlying beliefs about the rights of labor, as well as with the political necessities confronting the Democrats in 1946. His intemperate language in May should not be interpreted as a reversal of his longstanding commitment to collective bargaining. Given that the public was furious with labor, Truman's advocacy of harmonious solutions through use of fact-finding boards represented a prolabor position. After being criticized by liberals for agreeing to concessions to industry in the winter of 1945–1946, he became less willing to conciliate management. And, as always, the political equation was important to Truman. By vetoing the Case bill, he was actually initiating the so-called veto strategy, which would characterize his 1948 campaign.

The economic problems of the immediate postwar period caused Harry Truman grief with several groups at once. It seemed he could not win, as Barton Bernstein has written:

Whereas the politics of depression generally allowed the Roosevelt Administration, by bestowing benefits, to court interest groups and contribute to an economic upturn, the politics of inflation required a responsible government like Truman's to curb wages, prices, and profits and to deny the growing expectations of rival groups.

The Cold War Begins

Truman's role in the origins of the Cold War in 1945–1946, and in the ensuing hunt for "subversives" at home, has provoked considerable controversy among historians. Undeniably he brought staunchly anti-Communist views to the White House. It had been Senator Harry Truman, after all, who years earlier had pronounced on the Senate floor his fervent wish that Nazi Germany and Soviet Russia would chew each other to pieces on the battlefield. His antagonistic view of the Soviets was also evident in the dressing down he gave to Russian Foreign Minister Molotov upon their first meeting after Truman had become president in April 1945. Like Averell Harriman and others of FDR's more hard-nosed advisers, Truman viewed the Soviet Union as a "world bully." To many observers—particularly liberals, who took a relatively tolerant view of Soviet objectives—the new president's approach seemed in sharp contrast to Roosevelt's conciliatory attitude and demonstrated willingness to negotiate with Stalin.

Did Truman's approach in fact represent a shift in American policy regarding the Soviets? Daniel Yergin, in *Shattered Peace,* argues that it did. Roosevelt, according to Yergin, had operated on the basis of a number of "axioms" that essentially accepted (and respected) the reality of Soviet power and aimed to establish a stable international order that would take that power into account. But Truman, Yergin writes, "rejected the Roosevelt axioms in favor of a cluster of other assumptions . . . which reflected a general confusion and uncertainty about the objectives of the Soviet Union. . . ." In Truman's view, "The Russians were thought to have taken advantage of American generosity . . . ; further, they supposedly were breaking solemn agreements. But if the Russians were treated firmly, . . . they could be brought around. In other words, the Soviet Union could be made to accept a subsidiary role in the postwar world."

Yet, a strong case can be made that Truman neither intended nor effected an immediate reversal of Roosevelt's "strategy of cooperation" with the Soviets. In all likelihood, writes John Gaddis in *The United States and the Origins of the Cold War, 1941–1947,* Truman "thought he was carrying on Roosevelt's policies when he lectured Molotov [in April 1945] on Moscow's failure to keep the Yalta agreements." Adds Gaddis, "to view the new President's confrontation with Molotov as the opening move in a well-planned, long-range strategy for dealing with the Soviet Union is to presume a degree of foresight and consistency which simply was not present during the early days of the Truman administration." Although such key advisers as Harriman, Admiral William Leahy, and James Forrestal were pressing him toward a less conciliatory posture, Truman demurred because he perceived that American public opinion was not ready to accept such a redirection of policy toward an erstwhile ally.

If Truman's pragmatism led him to distrust the Soviets, his basically neighborly instincts moderated that distrust—at least for a time. "I'm not afraid of Russia," he wrote in his diary in mid-1945. "They've always been our friends and I can't see any reason why they shouldn't always be." Events, however, stiffened Truman's resolve to deal sternly with the Soviets.

The Cold War began at Alamogordo, New Mexico, on July 16, 1945. To accept this view, it is not necessary to believe that possession of the atomic bomb turned the United States to bullying other nations, specifically the Soviet Union. It is sufficient to note the significance that Truman and his top advisers ascribed to the bomb in connection with the timing of the Potsdam conference, and Truman's reaction at Potsdam when he received news of the successful test.

Apprehensive about his first face-to-face meeting with Stalin, scheduled for late July 1945, Truman readily adopted Secretary of War Henry L. Stimson's inclination: that the Potsdam conference should be scheduled to coincide with the bomb test so that the weapon could be played—in Stimson's words—as "a royal straight flush" in dealing with the Soviets. It proved infeasible to have the test actually occur before the agreed-upon opening of the Potsdam sessions; consequently, the American delegation learned while at Potsdam of the successful test. Once in possession of the good news from New Mexico, Truman mentioned the bomb only cryptically to Stalin, not inviting negotiation on the future of the deadly new technology, but instead presenting it as an implied threat. And so Stalin understood it.

The major issue after the bomb was used at Hiroshima and Nagasaki in August 1945, of course, was what to do about the atomic "secret": share it with the Soviets and others, in hopes of averting an eventual nuclear arms race, or guard it closely in order to retain a monopoly and the diplomatic leverage that went with it. Within Congress, there were strong pressures—especially from Republicans—to retain the secret. Leading Republican Senator Arthur Vandenberg, for example, termed it "unthinkable" to consider letting the Soviet Union take the secret of atomic technology "behind its blackout curtain." Meanwhile, public opinion was classically ambivalent. A Gallup poll in September 1945 indicated 82 percent of respondents expected other nations to develop atomic weapons, while 85 percent wanted the United States to keep a monopoly as long as it could.

Administration policy reflected this ostrich-like approach, even as it became more and more obvious that there was no secret to keep, and that the atomic monopoly seemed to be hindering diplomacy rather than helping. Yet the administration only halfheartedly pursued the idea of setting up an international commission for overseeing nuclear development. Truman's basic attitude was expressed in his remark to an associate in September: "When we get down to cases," he asked, "is any one of the Big Powers—are we?—going to give up these locks and bolts which are necessary to protect our house . . . against possible outlaw attack . . . until experience and good judgment say that the community is sufficiently stable . . . ? Clearly we are not. Nor are the Soviets. Nor is any country if it can help itself."

It would have been unrealistic to expect Truman to act much differently in the atmosphere that prevailed in 1945 and 1946. Critics of Truman's policies have maintained that the president should have taken greater risks in attempting to win over the Soviets by a more generous-minded atomic policy, but his decisions and actions should be seen in their full context. Pressure from Republican critics was important. Vandenberg's publicized conversion from isolationism to internationalism in early 1945 weakened isolationist forces in the GOP, but he and others continued to express strong suspicion of the Soviet Union. Republicans had engaged in "red baiting" in the 1944 campaign against Roosevelt, and after the war, party members hinted with increasing frequency at ties between suspected leftist domestic policies and "softness" on communism abroad. Truman, on shaky political ground anyway during his first year in office—and harboring his own innate distrust of Soviet motives—could hardly have been expected to resist this tide of criticism in Congress.

Increasingly, too, international developments underscored the wisdom of taking a hard line toward the Soviets. In February 1946, Stalin delivered a stridently anticapitalist speech; at the same time, the presence of Soviet troops in Iran as a force to induce oil concessions by the Iranians served to strengthen Truman's commitment to stand firm. The president's resolve was reinforced by a "long telegram" from U.S. Ambassador George Kennan in Moscow, vigorously condemning Soviet motives. Meanwhile, Vandenberg kept up the Republican drumfire, urging that the United States "abandon this miserable fiction, often encouraged by our fellow-travelers, that we somehow jeopardize the peace if our candor is as firm as Russia's always is." In March, British Prime Minister Winston Churchill's speech at Fulton, Missouri, in which he described an "iron curtain" descending over Europe, further heightened—and justified—the growing anti-Soviet sentiment.

In order to preempt Republican criticisms, Truman and Secretary of State James Byrnes took up a strategy termed "bipartisanship" in early 1946. Byrnes took Vandenberg along to four peace conferences during the year; more significantly, the administration did little to encourage Democratic opposition to Vandenberg in Michigan when he campaigned for reelection in the fall. Vandenberg's success in quieting the GOP was limited, though another important Republican—Thomas Dewey's chief foreign policy adviser, John Foster Dulles—in effect endorsed Truman's Soviet policies in a two-part *Life* magazine article published in June 1946.

The direction American foreign policy was taking led inevitably to a break between Truman and former Vice President Henry Wallace, who was serving as secretary of commerce. Wallace hoped to convert the president to a more conciliatory attitude toward the Soviets, but he was deceiving himself. In mid-March 1946, Wallace wrote a letter to the president recommending a new approach, built on the principle of economic cooperation. By criticizing Churchill's recent "iron curtain" speech, he placed himself in clear opposition to Truman. In late July, he sent the president another lengthy letter, warning of a possible new isolationism "masquerading as tough realism"; he emphasized that Russian actions had arisen from "reasonable . . . fear, suspicions, and distrust" of American actions. The president thanked Wallace and forwarded the letter to Secretary of State Byrnes.

The crisis came to a head when Wallace delivered what was ostensibly a Democratic campaign speech at New York City's Madison Square Garden on September 12, 1946. In it, his criticism of the GOP was overshadowed by his remarks concerning Truman's foreign policy. In presenting his own blueprint for world peace, Wallace came down as hard on the British as he did on the Russians. He added that Truman had read and agreed with his sentiments, implying that the president had approved the whole speech.

Both in his diary and in his later published memoirs, Truman denied that he had given careful attention to the speech ahead of time, claiming that Wallace had trapped him. Historians differ in their interpretations. For example, Norman Markowitz (*The Rise and Fall of the People's Century*) and Richard Walton (*Henry Wallace, Harry Truman, and the Cold War*) believe Truman had given a go-ahead to Wallace and then withdrawn it. Alonzo Hamby, however, offers a more convincing explanation in *Beyond the New Deal: Harry S. Truman and American Liberalism:*

Wallace met with the president on September 10 to discuss the address and at least two other topics. Subsequently, Truman claimed that they talked for only a few minutes, while Wallace asserted that they carefully examined the speech for "over an hour." (The White House appointment book scheduled Wallace for only fifteen minutes but it is possible that his stay ran overtime.) There can be no doubt that Truman, always a bit nervous with Wallace, did not give the address his close attention. It is equally certain that Wallace engaged in a bit of salesmanship which was less than candid. He especially emphasized the innocuous sentence, "I am neither anti-British nor pro-British, neither anti-Russian nor pro-Russian." When Truman expressed emphatic agreement . . . Wallace quickly secured his permission to mention their accord in the speech.

In fact, Wallace's speech was relatively moderate; it does not seem to have represented a conscious desire on his part for a public break with the president. But the congressional elections were imminent, and the episode threatened to undermine Democratic chances if left unresolved. Truman's response was to fire Wallace a few days later. This action lost Truman further ground with liberals, but to have allowed Wallace to stay would have cost Vandenberg's support and given the Republicans an issue in the 1946 campaigns. In any case, a break between Truman and Wallace would have occurred at some point; that it occurred in September 1946 reflected more the necessities of party politics than any other factor.

The 1946 Elections

Truman spent the first fifteen months or so of his presidency making mistakes and learning from them. He seemed weak and vacillating, and his popularity hit a low point during the period, both with the public and within his party. Liberals were increasingly disaffected, while southern conservatives were suspicious as a result of the twenty-one points the president had proposed a year earlier.

The nadir of Truman's political fortunes came in the fall of 1946. The Republicans enjoyed natural advantages in this first postwar electoral contest. In addition to problems resulting from the president's ineffectual record in labor-manage-ment matters, his apparent weakness as a legislative leader, and the normal tendency for the out-party to gain in off-year elections, the Democratic party seemed fragmented into liberal and conservative camps.

Most damaging to the Democrats was the rampant infla-tion that set in after the fight over extension of OPA ended in an ungraceful draw in fall 1946. As diversion of food to Europe to compensate for ravaged crops produced domestic shortages in the United States, the political situation became impossible for Truman. Confronted by public demonstrations against OPA and administration economic policies generally, the embit-tered president ended price controls on meat in mid-October. Privately, the president seethed, complaining that the people had "deserted" him "for a mess of pottage, a piece of beef—a side of bacon." He resolved that he could "no longer enforce a law [the people] won't support, botched and bungled by an unwilling Congress."

The stage was set for a rout of the Democrats in the No-vember elections. Truman, probably wisely, played a minor role during the campaign, but in so doing he confirmed the public impression of his weak leadership. Campaigning on the unsubtle theme "Had Enough?" the GOP won its predicted smashing victory. Picking up twelve seats in the Senate and fifty-five in the House, Republicans won control of both houses of Congress for the first time since 1930. Only four of eleven Democratic senators running for reelection outside the South won: Dennis Chavez of New Mexico, Harley Kilgore of West Virginia, Ernest McFarland of Arizona, and Joseph O'Ma-honey of Wyoming. In the House, the party lost over 40 per-cent of its seats outside Dixie. Republicans also won gover-norships in twenty-five nonsouthern states. A number of strong and outspoken personalities emerged in this Republican "Class of 1946," including Senators Joseph McCarthy of Wisconsin, William Knowland of California, John Bricker of Ohio, and William Jenner of Indiana. Among the many young GOP freshmen elected to the House was Richard M. Nixon of California.

The 1946 returns showed Democratic voter defections of almost every kind. In addition to a sharp falling off of support from liberals, the election saw a surge to the Republican party of more conservative, heavily Catholic voting groups that had supported FDR but were repelled by what they perceived as Wallace's pro-Communist leanings. Some Democratic candidates, fearing such a public perception, refused to allow Wallace to campaign for them at all, and Republican office seekers engaged in red baiting with impunity. Typical was the message of John Bricker, campaigning for the Senate in Ohio: "Bring on your New Deal, Communistic and subversive groups. . . . If we can't lick them in Ohio, America is lost anyway." The results established that both Ohio and the nation would remain safe from the Red threat.

The Democrats also ran into problems with two other parts of the New Deal coalition: white southerners and blacks. Southern conservatives were angry on several counts—including Truman's support for continuation of the wartime Fair Employment Practices Commission to guard against racial discrimination in employment; his opposition to state's rights to offshore oil; and his seemingly prolabor stance in vetoing the Case labor bill. Actual Democratic losses in the South, however, were small in 1946. On the other hand, urban blacks—put off by the white supremacist campaigns waged in 1946 by many Dixie Democrats—defected in significant numbers to the GOP. This was especially obvious in New York, Philadelphia, Detroit, and Chicago.

Historians have portrayed the 1946 elections as a disaster for the Democrats, but it is possible to take another view. The Democratic-controlled Congress Truman faced in 1945–1946 had not been very cooperative. "Between you and me," the president wrote Senator (later Supreme Court Justice) Sherman Minton just days after the elections, "I don't expect this Congress to be any worse than the one I had to deal with for the last two years." Now, at least, he could use an opposition-controlled Congress as a foil, presenting his administration and the Democratic party as friends of the people. In some ways, perhaps, the Democratic defeat in 1946 was a necessary step toward the party's surprising recovery in 1948.

The Politics of Containment

The newly Republican Congress was bound to have an impact on American foreign policy. Some GOP leaders had long held isolationist sentiments; a far greater number were strongly committed to reducing federal spending and skeptical of executive branch requests for money for any purpose, including defense and foreign policy. Administration efforts to counter Soviet pressures abroad were threatened also by congressional apathy. "I think we must admit the conclusion," wrote a State Department official in early 1947, "that Congress and the people of this country are not sufficiently aware of the character and dimensions of the crisis that impends, and of the measures that must be taken ... on a scale hitherto unimaginable—if disaster is to be avoided." Public suspicion of the Soviets might have been growing in the several months after World War II, but foreign policy and defense matters still held low priority for most Americans.

Yet the administration had resolved that Russian expansion must be blocked, and that the United States had to lead that effort. Therefore, when the British informed Truman in early 1947 that they could no longer afford the costs of shoring up the Greek government against military pressure from Communist insurgents, he seized the opportunity to enlist the support of Congress and the public for his hardening policies. Prior to consulting with congressional leaders on February 27, Truman had already decided to take up the British role. His appeal to Congress on March 12 for a $400 million aid package for Greece and Turkey, grounded in harsh and uncompromising language, was quickly dubbed the Truman Doctrine. "At the present moment in world history," Truman told Congress, "nearly every nation must choose between alternative ways of

life. The choice is too often not a free one. . . . I believe that
it must be the policy of the United States to support free peo-
ples who are resisting attempted subjugation by armed minorities or by outside pressures." The president closed with a
warning: "If we falter in our leadership, we may endanger the
peace of the world—and we shall surely endanger the welfare
of our own Nation."

The importance of Truman's words was indisputable. "The
Truman Doctrine speech," Richard Freeland has written (*The
Truman Doctrine and the Origins of McCarthyism*), "was an
official pronouncement of unusual historical significance. . . .
[I]t was to become the seminal declaration of American foreign
policy in the postwar period."

The administration proposal drew opposition from all directions. Conservative Republicans objected to its expense,
and Robert Taft in particular feared that it implied adoption
of a "spheres of influence" approach to the world. Thomas E.
Dewey, GOP presidential candidate in 1944, spoke for a growing contingent in his party when he criticized Truman for
ignoring the plight of China while sinking such extensive resources into Europe. Liberals, on the other hand, viewed the
program as too belligerent; Eleanor Roosevelt called instead
for "a high-level effort to settle matters directly with Stalin,"
while Henry Wallace condemned the administration for taking
an overtly anti-Soviet attitude.

Truman's crisis tactics worked, however. The Greek and
Turkish aid bill passed quickly and easily, 67 to 23 in the
Senate and 287 to 107 in the House. Vandenberg, chairman
of the Foreign Relations Committee in the Republican-controlled Senate, played an important—perhaps a decisive—role
in the outcome, as he was to do in the case of many other
administration measures over the next year or so. But he, too,
was disgruntled, writing to a former colleague in late March
that "these 'crises' never reach Congress until they have developed to a point where Congressional discretion is pathet-
ically restricted."

A theoretical rationale for the administration's new policy

soon appeared in the form of a lengthy document authored by Department of State policy analyst George Kennan. Published anonymously in the summer issue of *Foreign Affairs,* Kennan's piece developed the theory of "containment," essentially a patient, flexible, and defensive response to inevitable Soviet pressures around the world. The containment strategy directly reflected the views of Secretary of the Navy James Forrestal—"godfather of the article," according to Daniel Yergin. Forrestal was known for his tough views toward Russia; his influence within the administration was therefore of more than passing importance.

The new, tougher U.S. policy was buttressed by creation of a strengthened national security apparatus. In February 1947, after forcing bickering service representatives to compromise on a single proposal, Truman forwarded an omnibus bill that became law in July 1947 as the National Security Act. The measure recognized the army, navy, and air force as coequal departments, all under a civilian secretary of defense. In September, Forrestal assumed that post. The act also set up three new security-related agencies: the Central Intelligence Agency (CIA), to coordinate all overseas intelligence-gathering activities, analyze the information gained, and disseminate it on a "need to know" basis; the National Security Council (NSC), a presidential advisory council on matters related to the integration of foreign and military policies; and the National Security Resources Board (NSRB), a civilian-headed unit to advise the president on the impact of security considerations on the economy. Taken together, the provisions of the National Security Act represented a significant enhancement of the executive branch and, as later historians would note, institutionalization of the "Cold War State." The bill passed by voice vote in both houses.

At the same time the administration unveiled the containment doctrine and strengthened the national security apparatus, it also devised a comprehensive approach to the task of rebuilding Western Europe and blocking Communist inroads there. The proposal was eventually known as the Marshall Plan, or European Recovery Program (ERP).

As rumors circulated on Capitol Hill that the president was planning a gigantic five-year program to prop up European economies, costing perhaps $20 billion, Republicans reacted negatively. On being apprised of the emerging proposal, Vandenberg exclaimed to his informant: "either you are wrong or this government is out of its mind. Any plan of that size is out of the question." The administration adopted an effective strategy to gain approval of the ERP. Eschewing the primarily humanitarian, open economy arguments that characterized Secretary of State George C. Marshall's public introduction of the plan in June 1947, the White House opted to sell the idea as an extension of the Truman Doctrine in order to capitalize on strong anti-Communist sentiment in the GOP. This tack was made easier when the Soviets and their East European satellite nations declined an invitation to participate in the proposed ERP.

For political reasons, Truman kept a low profile and allowed his recently appointed secretary of state, revered as the architect of the American military victory in World War II, to serve as public symbol and sponsor of the program. To assist in lobbying efforts, a high-powered private-sector Committee for the Marshall Plan was set up, including among its influential members former cabinet members Henry L. Stimson and Robert Patterson. Meanwhile, Undersecretary of State Dean Acheson assiduously courted Congress.

But for all these efforts, the Marshall Plan did not enjoy smooth sailing through Congress. Moderate GOP Senator Henry Cabot Lodge of Massachusetts, a strong internationalist, mirrored the depth of opposition, concluding after one committee session on the program that it was "the biggest damned interference in internal affairs [of other nations] that there has ever been in history." Other Republicans were even less restrained. From the left, too, the Marshall Plan drew fire. By late 1947, Henry Wallace, continuing his progress along the path of alienation from the administration, abandoned his original support for the measure, describing it as merely a "containment device."

But Western Europe desperately wanted the aid, and Truman doggedly pressed for passage. Despite Republican foot dragging, both houses passed an interim aid bill in December. Simultaneously, Truman submitted to Congress legislation establishing the ERP. By March 1948, the president—helped by news of a Communist coup in Czechoslovakia—charged that the Soviets were blocking world peace, and he lumped the ERP with his other national security requests, including universal military training and revival of selective service. In April, the Marshall Plan authorization bill passed easily, and two months later, Congress approved the appropriation. Vandenberg's invaluable help in shepherding the ERP through the Senate vindicated administration efforts to court him through nearly continuous consultation during the preceding months.

Senator Vandenberg also helped the administration extend the American commitment to European collective security in another way, securing passage of a Senate resolution bearing his name that sanctioned United States participation in a regional security pact. The Vandenberg Resolution, adopted in June, laid the groundwork for the North Atlantic Treaty Organization (NATO), the first instance of American participation in a peacetime alliance since the days of George Washington.

Vandenberg's assistance and the increasing Republican acquiescence in Truman's foreign policy initiatives (with respect to Europe, at least) did not signify complete cooptation of the GOP by the administration, as subsequent events would make all too clear. Observers, however, chose to read the temporary convergence of opinion between the administration and congressional Republicans as signaling a new era in foreign policy making. Picking up the self-serving language employed by the leading participants, the press announced the triumph of bipartisanship—a term which seemed to connote something above "mere" party considerations. It was true that the final votes on several important foreign aid measures in 1947 and early 1948 were lopsided, with few Republicans recorded in opposition. This reflected, in the words of Susan Hartmann (*Truman and the Eightieth Congress*), a "consensus on foreign policy [that] . . . was remarkable." Other historians have tended to agree, "[T]he emotional and political forces and the patterns of belief—what in aggregate might be called the 'Cold War consensus,' " writes Freeland, "were quite fully developed by early 1948."

But was this consensus, or was it the inevitable result of political conflict and compromise? A careful reading of events in 1947–1948 suggests that Truman won grudging GOP support by manipulation, fashioning his arguments to capitalize on the red-baiting mentality common to so many formerly isolationist Republicans who could not have been won over by traditional internationalist appeals. While Truman's containment policies ultimately derived from his understanding of the international situation, the strident anticommunism of the GOP stimulated forcefulness in the president's presentation—a style that, in turn, made it difficult for Republicans to vote against the measures comprising containment.

Such an interpretation makes sense, especially in light of parallel developments relating to internal security in the years 1947–1948. In the summer of 1946 Republicans and conservative Democrats alike pressured Truman to take on the rising Communist menace. Revelations in 1945 of the leaking of secret State Department documents to the academic journal *Amerasia* were partially responsible for these pressures, but in the case of Republicans they flowed naturally from the red baiting of the 1944 campaign. GOP sniping intensified once the congressional campaigns of 1946 heated up. At the same time, anti-Communist statements emanated also from powerful union leaders, such as Congress of Industrial Organizations (CIO) head Philip Murray.

Truman's response to these pressures was predictable. Immediately after the Republican victory in the November elections, he appointed a Temporary Commission on Employee Loyalty to assess the nature and scope of the problem. Four months later, by Executive Order 9835, he acted on the commission's recommendations, establishing a Loyalty Review Board within the Civil Service Commission. Daniel Yergin has succinctly summarized the forces at work: ". . . these steps were not part of a campaign to whip up domestic fervor, but rather, at least as viewed from the White House, efforts to contain such passions and to forestall possible efforts by the Eightieth Congress to manipulate them for partisan purposes." Rejecting the contention that President Truman in effect initiated "McCarthyism," Yergin concludes, "It is a very different matter to try to calm things down rather than to stir them up."

Whatever the administration's motives, however, its actions served to heighten concern over internal security. The loyalty program, once set in motion, grew rapidly; by the end of 1948, there were 150 departmental and regional loyalty boards in operation. As a conciliatory gesture to conservative Republicans, Truman appointed one of their own, Seth Richardson, to head the parent Review Board. Meanwhile, Attorney General Tom Clark compiled a list of "subversive" organizations; after the list was made public in late 1947, the designated organizations were hampered considerably in their political activities. The attorney general also pressed forward with an investigation of the Communist Party USA (CPUSA), hoping to build a case against it under the Smith Act of 1940, which made it a crime to advocate the overthrow of the government even if no action occurred. But the attorney general could not move fast enough to please critics in the Republican party. One of them, Representative J. Parnell Thomas of New Jersey, chairman of the House Committee on Un-American Activities (HUAC), insisted that Clark "immediately crack down on the Moscow-directed fifth column operating in the United States." Criticisms by two prominent conservative Republicans, Senator Styles Bridges of New Hampshire and Representative John Taber of New York, also were instrumental in forcing the State Department to retire China expert John

Carter Vincent and to dismiss summarily ten other employees for disloyalty.

Public opinion kept pace. Polls revealed that in early 1948, 10 percent of the public thought the CPUSA would soon "dominate the country," and an additional 35 percent believed the party already "controlled important segments of the economy." Dramatic charges leveled by such ex-Communists as Elizabeth Bentley and Whittaker Chambers thus found a receptive public audience.

By the spring of 1948, Truman was concerned that anticommunism had grown to excessive dimensions in the country. In May, he dismissed the dangers posed by the CPUSA, saying he did not think "the splinter parties do any harm." And he greeted with stony silence a legislative proposal by Representative Karl Mundt of HUAC, the Communist Control Act of 1948. But in a sense it was too late for Truman. Having chosen to compete with the GOP in two areas that were traditionally the preserve of Republicans, internal security and domestic communism, he had invited the GOP to hold him accountable, and plenty of Republicans were eager to oblige. As Speaker Joseph Martin promised in his Lincoln Day address, internal security would be an issue for the GOP in the 1948 election:

The New Deal Administration knew full well the intentions of the Kremlin. We Republicans warned of the march of communism for ten or twelve years. We told the nation the communists were sneaking into high government places. Now it is going to take a Republican administration to clear out the fifth columnists and traitors from the government structure. Those who insisted for years on keeping them there will never do the job.

Partisan warfare over internal security underscored the illusory nature of bipartisanship in foreign policy. Moreover, the growing disharmony over national security was only part of the story. Although Truman maneuvered Congress into approving his containment policies in 1947, he enjoyed no such good fortune in domestic matters. Here the Republican majorities proved intransigent, producing a bitter standoff between Capitol Hill and the White House. In such an atmosphere, how could one expect cooperation on foreign policy for any extended period? As White House aide Clark Clifford noted in the strategy memorandum he prepared for the president in November 1947, "To expect reasonableness and partnership in foreign affairs while guerilla warfare is going on in domestic matters is to expect that politicians overnight have become more than the mortal beings they are." No such transformation had occurred, as events of the coming election year would demonstrate.

Truman and the Eightieth Congress

The guerilla warfare to which Clark Clifford referred extended along many domestic fronts. While Truman paid increasing attention to problems of the emerging Cold War, the initiative on matters at home fell to the Republican-controlled Congress. As it turned out, Truman could not have designed a scenario more beneficial to the Democrats. The GOP's new majority status quickly exposed its internal divisions, and the two most significant domestic measures passed by the Eightieth Congress, the Taft-Hartley Act and a tax reduction bill, could be cited by the Democrats as proof of the GOP's insensitivity to the common man. Combined with the political advantages accruing to Truman from Cold War developments, Congress's actions stimulated a Democratic revival.

For the first few months of 1947—a period dominated by concern over the worsening Cold War—Truman and Congress maintained a wary peace. The president refrained from pressing his liberal programs on Congress, partly to avert backlash against his foreign policy proposals, but also for the strategic reason suggested by Secretary of Commerce Averell Harriman that divisive proposals that "would permit the president to make political capital by lambasting the Republicans should be put off until 1948," when such charges could benefit his campaign for reelection. Then in late May, with help from southern Democrats, GOP leaders secured a major tax cut, featuring large reductions for those in higher income brackets, as well as lesser cuts for lower-income Americans. On June 16, Truman vetoed the proposed cut, emphasizing the risks of inflation and excessive federal debt, and charging that the bill was "neither fair not equitable." The veto was sustained—though barely—in the House, but in April 1948, Congress succeeded in passing another, more moderate tax cut over a second veto.

In keeping with their promises in the 1946 campaign, the Republicans also sought a law to correct the "excesses" of the Wagner Act and to weaken labor unions. Antiunion legislators cited Truman's own earlier requests as a basis for their bills, but the president—in contrast to his rash behavior during the 1946 railroad strike—spoke out against overreaction. "We must not," he warned, "in order to punish a few labor leaders, pass vindictive laws which will restrict the proper rights of the rank and file of labor." Despite this posturing, what followed was probably exactly what he wanted: passage of the stringent (but not impossible) Taft-Hartley Act over his veto. The law, wrote constitutional scholar Edward Corwin a year after its passage, "could have been made a better one if Mr. Truman and the people who were promoting the measure had gotten together and discussed matters with the purpose in mind of arriving at the best solution." Instead, Truman chose to engage in confrontational politics for his own tactical purposes, further exacerbating the climate for labor-management relations.

Republican strategy on the labor bill also helped ensure confrontation. Representative Fred Hartley of New Jersey, chief sponsor of the bill in the more conservative lower house, packed his proposal full of antiunion provisions to leave leeway for trade-offs without endangering the basic purpose of the bill. When Senate forces, led by Taft, excised certain provisions, therefore, the final result was still perceived, as Hartley intended, as aiming at the heart of the union movement. Organized labor lobbied furiously, and White House mail ran overwhelmingly in favor of a veto. Truman complied with a sharp veto message on June 20, but was overridden by stunning votes of 331–83 in the House, and 68–25 in the Senate.

The Taft-Hartley episode was symbolically important, even if its provisions (outlawing of the closed shop and secondary boycott; a mandated eighty-day "cooling off" period before strikes; requirement of anti-Communist affidavits from union officials; and allowance for state right-to-work laws, to name the most important) proved less damaging to labor than anticipated. Its passage over Truman's veto mirrored the clash between the two parties, one the friend of the working man, the other not. It made little difference now that Truman had earlier vacillated on labor-management issues, or that the bill had fewer teeth than was commonly thought. An important result of the act was a dramatic increase in the politicization of labor. As A. H. Raskin wrote later, Taft-Hartley "got unions into politics on a year-round basis"; the outcome of the struggle also reaffirmed Truman's belief that confrontation was politically productive.

The Eightieth Congress wanted not only to reduce federal intervention into the private sector, but also to reassert its authority with respect to the White House. One way Congress could do this, of course, was by having its way with legislation—including, if necessary, overriding vetoes. A more direct step, however, was the effort in early 1947 by Republicans in both houses to adopt a Constitutional amendment limiting a president to two terms. Introduced in January, the proposed amendment passed in March, after only perfunctory hearings and floor debate. Voting on the amendment was highly partisan: in the House, where the final tally was 285–121, Republicans voted unanimously (238–0) in favor; in the Senate, Republicans were again unanimous (46–0) in their support, as Democrats divided 13 for, 23 opposed. Passage of the proposed amendment, which took five years to achieve ratification, fulfilled Republican platform planks from 1940 and 1944. The Eightieth Congress had avenged itself against FDR, although Truman was exempted from the terms of the amendment.

Truman also encountered congressional resistance in another area where he sought action—civil rights. Considerable opposition, of course, came from his own party. Though the Democrats had benefited from strong black support at the polls since Roosevelt's reelection in 1936, they did little over the next decade to advance the cause of black civil rights. But the confrontation with the evils of Nazi racism, the migration of blacks throughout the nation during World War II (and thus their greater presence in areas where they could and did vote), and a rising level of black assertiveness all suggested to Truman the wisdom of responding to blacks' needs.

As in the case of anticommunism, Truman's motives in the area of civil rights have been variously interpreted. On the one hand, William C. Berman (*The Politics of Civil Rights in the Truman Administration*) has painted a critical portrait, depicting Truman as going no further than was expedient, and then only for cynical reasons. Citing episodes from Truman's years in the Senate, Berman describes his "political and personal ambivalence" on such matters. "You know I am against this bill," Truman is quoted as remarking to a southern senator about a 1938 antilynching bill, "but if it comes to a vote, I'll have to vote for it. All my sympathies are with you but the Negro vote in Kansas City and St. Louis is too important." Blacks had not been happy with Truman's selection as Roosevelt's running mate in 1944, and in his first several months in the White House, he did nothing to increase their enthusiasm for him.

But most historians subscribe to the view that, as Alonzo Hamby succinctly states, "Truman displayed a belief in elementary justice for minority groups." Though his commitment to fairness and his instinct for political advantage led him only gradually to act, criticisms surfaced among Dixie legislators during his first year in office. In response to even limited presidential support for civil rights, for example, Georgia Senator Walter F. George grumbled in January 1946: "If this is all that Harry Truman has to offer, God help the Democratic Party in 1946 and 1948."

Truman continued to avoid a clash with his southern party

colleagues through the fall of 1946, but once the disastrous campaign was over he tacked in a different direction. In December he set up a twelve-member Committee on Civil Rights to review the whole spectrum of racial problems in the country. Certainly, Truman was motivated by genuine concern about the way black veterans were being treated, but the timing of his action may have been partly dictated by his need to recoup the losses he had suffered on the Left as a result of Henry Wallace's firing. Moreover, Republican campaigns in 1946 had included many promises to blacks, and the National Association for the Advancement of Colored People (NAACP) was openly suggesting the possibility of a massive black defection to the GOP if some of those promises were kept. It seemed unlikely, however, that the Republicans would do much. "I'll be frank with you," Speaker Martin told an audience of black Republicans. "We are not going to pass an FEPC [Fair Employment Practices Commission] bill, but it has nothing to do with the Negro vote. We are supported by New England and Middle Western Industrialists who would stop their contributions if we passed a law that would compel them to stop religious as well as racial discrimination in employment. . . . [W]e may as well be realistic."

So long as administration support for civil rights remained only theoretical, southern Democrats and Republican critics kept quiet on the issue. When Truman delivered a ringing pro-civil rights speech before an NAACP rally in June 1947, however—insisting that "each man must be guaranteed equality of opportunity"—the unease of his critics increased. In October, release of the report of the president's committee, *To Secure These Rights,* galvanized the growing opposition. Schism seemed inevitable if Truman were to push for the committee's ambitious civil rights recommendations—for example, the elimination of discrimination in public facilities and education.

The president's troubles with southerners over civil rights and his standoff with the Republican-controlled Congress were compounded by the estrangement of more progressive-minded

Democrats. Following Wallace's dismissal in September 1946, a Conference of Progressives convened to reaffirm support for the principles of Roosevelt's 1944 "Economic Bill of Rights" and to plan strategy for the election of a progressive Congress that fall. Rumors circulated that the gatherings foreshadowed establishment of a "national liberal organization."

At the end of December 1946, the long-waited organization appeared as the Progressive Citizens of America (PCA). Almost immediately there arose a countermovement of liberals unsympathetic to the heretical foreign policy views of Wallace and the PCA: Americans for Democratic Action (ADA), chartered in January 1947, announced its twin aims as support of the domestic policies of Roosevelt and Truman and commitment to containing the Communist threat. A number of prominent union leaders supported the ADA, which in the words of journalist Elmer Davis seemed a "government-in-exile" set up to thwart the will of the Eightieth Congress. Formation of ADA, however, could not quell dissent from the Left. During 1947, Wallace grew more outspoken in his critique of Truman's policies and his followers became more ambitious.

Administration supporters worried about the former vice president's potential impact in 1948. "There is no question that Wallace has captured the imagination of a strong segment of the American public," Democratic National Committee official Gael Sullivan wrote to Clark Clifford in early June 1947. "Adequate thought should be given to decide whether Wallace is wanted back and something should be done about it before he gets himself too far committed to a Third party." Proposal of the Marshall Plan and the president's veto of the Taft-Hartley Act seemed to check temporarily the threat of a bolt by the party's left wing, but Wallace himself was not mollified. By late summer he was contemplating a third party.

While Wallace delayed in declaring his formal presidential candidacy, White House strategists were kept guessing. Clifford's tactical memorandum of mid-November 1947 included a major subsection entitled "The Insulation of Henry Wallace," in which he advised that "some lines should be kept out so that if the unpredictable Henry finally sees the light and can be talked into supporting the Administration, he will have a handy rope to climb back on the bandwagon—if he is wanted."

But Wallace's declaration of candidacy on December 27, 1947, rendered it difficult for the administration to keep any lines open to him. After discussing the problems of racial discrimination, inflation and worker unrest, he moved on to foreign policy, portraying Truman as a warmonger:

The luke warm liberals sitting on two chairs say, "why throw away your vote?" I say a vote for a new party in 1948 will be the most valuable vote you ever have cast or ever will cast. The bigger the peace vote in 1948, the more definitely the world will know that the United States is not behind the bi-partisan reactionary war policy which is dividing the world into two armed camps and making inevitable the day when American soldiers will be lying in their Arctic suits in the Russian snow. There is no real fight between a Truman and a Republican. Both stand for a policy which opens the door to war in our lifetime and makes war certain for our children.

The Election of 1948

Election year 1948 promised to be trying for Harry S. Truman. The civil rights issue threatened to cause at least as much trouble as the rift over foreign policy that had led to Wallace's defection. The report of the president's civil rights commission, *To Secure These Rights,* may have gone further than Truman had anticipated, but in February 1948, he took the report's argument to Congress, delivering the first presidential message to focus solely on civil rights. His speech angered southerners. "This much is certain," rumbled Mississippi Senator James Eastland, "if the present Democratic leadership is right, then Calhoun and Jefferson were wrong." Bills proposing a permanent Fair Employment Practices Commission and making lynching a federal crime were introduced, but the conservative coalition of southern Democrats and Republicans kept them from reaching the floor, and Democratic Senate

Leader Alben Barkley (Kentucky) refused to sponsor an omnibus civil rights proposal drafted by the administration. Nevertheless, Truman refrained from making civil rights a major thrust in his criticisms of the Eightieth Congress.

While Republicans hoped that the Democrats would chew each other up on civil rights, South Carolina Governor Strom Thurmond chaired an ad hoc committee of the Southern Governors' Conference that aimed to get the administration to compromise on the issue. Responding for the administration, Senator Howard McGrath of Rhode Island suggested that the weak 1944 party platform plank might serve as a model for 1948, but Thurmond and his colleagues were not placated, remarking that "the South was no longer in the bag." In mid-March, seven Dixie governors issued a call for southerners to vote in the fall only for candidates who opposed civil rights legislation. Meanwhile, black voters also flexed their muscles. On March 27, 1948, a group of twenty black organizations warned publicly that blacks' votes could provide the "balance of power" in seventeen states.

Truman's task was staggering. In David Garson's words, the president "had to keep Wallace isolated, . . . keep Negro voters in the Democratic column, and . . . insure that the revolt in Dixie could be contained" (*The Democratic Party and the Politics of Sectionalism, 1941–1948*). There was talk among Democrats of dumping Truman and nominating someone such as General Dwight D. Eisenhower or perhaps Justice William O. Douglas. Former New Dealer Harold Ickes, who had earlier resigned from Truman's cabinet, wrote to tell Truman that he had "the choice of retiring voluntarily and with dignity, or of being driven out of office by a disillusioned and indignant citizenry." The *New Republic* trumpeted, "As a candidate for President, Harry S. Truman should quit."

Truman refused to be intimidated. "For the next four years there will be a Democrat in the White House," he told a gathering of Young Democrats in May, "and you are looking at him." On June 3, he set out on a two-week, fifteen-state, whistle-stop tour through the West, during which he castigated the GOP-controlled Congress. Blaming the voters for their folly in electing Republicans two years earlier, Truman told a Spokane audience: "You deserve it. Now, if you let that sort of situation continue . . . I won't have any sympathy with you."

On June 21, the Democratic convention opened in Philadelphia. Attempting to avoid an open rupture in the party, the administration backed a civil rights plank identical to that of 1944. The tactic failed utterly; the southerners were not mollified, and the liberals revolted. Led by young Minnesota firebrand Hubert Humphrey, a candidate for the Senate in 1948, the pro–civil rights forces secured a narrow majority (651½ to 581½) for an amendment specifically praising Truman's sweeping civil rights proposals of early 1948. Immediately, the entire Mississippi delegation and half of Alabama's left the convention. Truman was then nominated easily, and Senator Barkley was chosen as his running mate. Deciding to take advantage of the galvanizing effect of the successful liberal revolt, the president delivered an electrifying acceptance speech. He promised to call the Eightieth Congress back into special session and to smoke the Republicans out on the major issues before the election.

Thomas E. Dewey, widely viewed as the inevitable Republican nominee, quipped that the special session would be "cruel and inhuman punishment" for both himself and Congress. Having beaten back primary challenges from former Governor Harold Stassen of Minnesota and derailed the candidacies of Robert Taft and California's Governor Earl Warren, Dewey won his party's nomination in a lackluster convention that then selected Warren as his running mate. Party conservatives were unenthusiastic, to say the least.

Still, the Republican party appeared monolithic in comparison to the factionalized Democrats. Already deserted by Wallace's followers, the newly nominated president now faced a bolt by southerners. After the Philadelphia convention, some 6,000 disaffected Dixie Democrats gathered in Birmingham and, in a revivalistic setting, selected a ticket consisting of Governors Strom Thurmond and Fielding Wright (Mississippi). The objective of the State's Rights Democrats, as they styled themselves, was not to found a permanent new party, but to gain leverage in the electoral college so that they could press their civil rights views on the rest of the party. Wiser heads among the "Dixiecrats"—including Thurmond—saw the need to construct a campaign broader than mere recalcitrance on civil rights, but the splinter party never succeeded in developing a positive program, or in raising an adequate campaign treasury.

The collective mood of the Dixiecrats was sour. If the president won, Senator Eastland told a Memphis rally in September, "our traditions and our culture will be destroyed and mongrelized by the mongrels of the East." Truman's issuance of Executive Orders 9980 and 9981 in late July, barring discrimination in federal employment and beginning desegregation of the armed forces, confirmed the worst fears of southerners. For the first time since Reconstruction, civil rights would be a major issue in a presidential campaign.

The Wallace Progressives convened in late July, the third party conclave to be held in Philadelphia during that hot summer. The delegates nominated Wallace for president and chose Idaho Senator Glen Taylor, a colorful singer of cowboy ballads, for the second spot on their national ticket. It was an idealistic—and distinctly amateur—crusade. The more than 3,200 delegates and alternates in attendance at the convention included only two congressmen and one senator (Taylor). By this time, however, the challenge posed by Wallace had diminished. One reason was the obvious influence of Communists within Progressive ranks—an influence which Wallace, incredibly, dismissed as politically unimportant. "If they want to support me," the former vice president remarked, "I can't stop them." By the fall, the steam had gone out of the Progressive campaign.

Events abroad conspired to make the "Communist issue" especially harmful to Wallace's cause, and beneficial to Truman's. Stimulated, perhaps, by the progress being made toward implementation of the Marshall Plan in late 1947, the Soviet

Union stepped up its aggressiveness in Europe. American intelligence reports spoke of the Communists' "concerted campaign of disorders, strikes, and sabotage in France and Italy," violence intensified in Greece, and—in February 1948—the democratic government of Czechoslovakia fell under Soviet control. Truman responded briskly. On March 17, he addressed Congress on the "Threat to the Freedom of Europe," calling for prompt implementation of the ERP, adoption of universal military training, and revival of the draft. Before the year was out, Congress passed the ERP appropriations and restored selective service, but the most important result of Truman's March speech was its public impact. The president has precisely captured the public mood of growing impatience and determination to block Soviet expansionism. Instead of being seen as a pitiable, vacillating caretaker, Harry Truman transformed his image to that of world leader.

Truman's new image was enhanced by his cool, firm-handed response in June when the Russians blocked western access to Berlin. The dramatic American airlift of goods into that beleaguered city, which lasted two years before succeeding in reopening it to the West, kept the Cold War issue alive throughout the 1948 campaign. These events, which Truman could not have orchestrated even had he wanted to, proved the wisdom of the political analysis passed on to Truman by aide Clark Clifford in November 1947. Urging the president to "assume . . . leadership on foreign policy," Clifford had commented sagely that there was "considerable political advantage to the Administration in its battle with the Kremlin."

Dewey and the Republicans might have managed to capitalize on the Cold War issue by flaying Truman for allowing it to degenerate to such a state, but they consciously chose not to. This decision to exclude foreign policy issues from the campaign was probably a serious political error, though it is impossible to know for certain how voters would have responded to partisan criticisms of the president's handling of foreign policy in the atmosphere of 1948. Dewey's main reason for not attacking, however, was his utter confidence that he would win—a view shared by virtually all observers. The Gallup and Roper polls in August and September showed the New Yorker receiving nearly half of the vote, with Truman's share varying from a low of 31 percent to a high of 39 percent. The smug and detached Dewey—described by Robert Donovan (*Conflict and Crisis*) as "too egotistical, too lordly, too overbearing, too didactic, too cold to like easily"—did not even begin to campaign until September 19. His tone of quiet reasonableness—largely lacking specific content—reinforced the public's perception of him as emotionless and calculating. Walt Kelly, creator of the popular cartoon strip *Pogo,* tellingly depicted the Republican candidate as a tiny robot with a human head. During the course of the campaign, Dewey made only about half the number of stops that Truman did.

"Thomas Elusive Dewey," as the caustic Harold Ickes dubbed him, was especially vague in his references to the Eightieth Congress. The special session called by Truman, begun on July 26, puttered its way to nowhere, adjourning by mid-August without enacting any major legislation. "I would say it was entirely a 'do-nothing' session," Truman remarked at his August 12 press conference. "I think that's a good name for the 80th Congress." The special session had been a political masterstroke by the president, confronting Dewey with the dilemma of trying to lead it from outside or totally dissociating himself from it. The Republican candidate did neither, all but ignoring the record of his party in Congress during the campaign and allowing the increasingly buoyant Truman to claim that his rival's campaign was giving a new meaning to the initials GOP: "Grand Old Platitudes."

The president, meanwhile, ran an effusive, energetic campaign, traveling nearly 22,000 miles, giving 275 speeches, and evoking from admiring audiences the response, "Give 'em hell, Harry." As Clifford's strategy memo had advised, Truman focused on the urban North, trying to appeal to the more liberal of his constituents. Taking a pragmatic view of the Dixiecrats' strength in the Deep South, he made only a few stops in that region and cemented his hold on the black vote by becoming the first Democratic presidential candidate ever to deliver a campaign speech in Harlem. His appeal to liberals was both blunt and consistent. He told organized labor that a GOP victory would lead to extreme antiunion actions, and won outright endorsement by the Congress of Industrial Organizations (CIO) and the American Federation of Labor (AFL), whose efforts (and money) proved enormously helpful to Democrats in several key states. During the course of the campaign, the president revived most of his liberal reform proposals of three years earlier, calling for rigid farm price supports, federal aid to education, increases in the minimum wage and in Social Security benefits, broad-gauge public power projects, and enactment of the omnibus civil rights program. Extending an olive branch to would-be defectors from the faltering Wallace campaign, he declared in a speech in Los Angeles: "This is the hour for the liberal forces of America to unite. . . . I call on all liberals and progressives to stand up and be counted for democracy."

In the face of contrary evidence from the polls, Truman remained serenely optimistic, a feeling shared by his running mate, Barkley. Such hopefulness seemed ill-founded, however. The Democrats were troubled throughout the campaign by shortages in funds; on occasion the national chairman had to hand-carry cash to broadcasting studios in order to pay for air time. On the eve of the election, the media unanimously forecast defeat for the president. *Life,* preparing for a new administration, ran an eight-page story on Dewey in its November 1 issue. The country, *Life* announced, "was about to ditch Truman and take Dewey for reasons that involved the brain as well as the emotions." Final preelection polls by those who were still bothering with them showed Dewey winning a minimum of 350 electoral votes.

Truman's narrow victory over Dewey was therefore seen as an upset by contemporaries—"the most astonishing political upset in modern times," Irwin Ross calls it (*The Loneliest Campaign*). The now-famous picture of Truman holding up a copy of the erroneous *Chicago Tribune* front page bearing the headline "Dewey Defeats Truman" captured the moment. The results were close: Truman won just over 24 million popular votes to Dewey's nearly 22 million, with Thurmond and Wallace each winning 1.1 million; in the electoral college, Truman's margin was 303–189, with 39 votes going to Thurmond. The Democrats also recaptured control of Congress, with margins of 54–42 in the Senate and 263–171 in the House.

Pollsters and commentators alike were stunned. "I can't help but get a good chuckle out of this," cracked Wilfred Funk, former editor of the *Literary Digest,* a magazine whose demise had been hastened by its forecast of an Alf Landon victory in 1936. The much-respected polls of Gallup, Roper, and Crossley had all failed; within days after the election, the Social Science Research Council assigned a committee to see how they could have been so wrong. There had been some sampling errors, the committee eventually concluded, but the biggest problem was that the pollsters had stopped counting noses too far in advance of the election.

But was Truman's victory an upset in any meaningful sense? The winning coalition, as Ross has written, "bore a remarkable resemblance to the design sketched by Clark Clifford" in 1947, and to Truman's own majority in his 1940 Missouri Senate race. Moreover, the 1948 vote mirrored the majority forged by Franklin D. Roosevelt twelve years earlier, which had carried the Democrats to victory again in 1940 and 1944. So much did Truman's 1948 coalition of rural West and urban East, organized labor, big-city blacks, and southern whites (at least outside the Deep South) resembled FDR's that one commentator described the results as "a testament to a dead man's vision." Herbert Parmet, in *The Democrats Since FDR,* calls the victory "a reprieve" for the party, in light of developments of the 1950s, noting that it was "a tribute to the persistence of the New Deal appeal" that lacked real substance. "Only among black Americans," Parmet concludes, "was the [Democratic] gain not built on sand." The authors of a sophisticated quantitative study, *Transformations of the American Party System,* Everett C. Ladd, Jr., and Charles Hadley, echo this view, calling the 1948 election "a curious hangover, a contest out of keeping with the larger sociopolitical realities of the time." Ladd and Hadley describe the Truman-Dewey contest as a "class-salient" election, which the incumbent won by his " 'bloody shirt' campaign—labeling the Republicans the party of Depression."

Certainly the triumph of the Truman-Barkley ticket took the nation by surprise, but it was no political aberration. Had pollsters continued on the job until the election, they could easily have detected the reemergence of the New Deal coalition, minus the Dixiecrat defectors. To view the election as a "curious hangover" in which voters were responding to Pavlovian stimuli rather than real issues, or to depict Truman's coalition as "built on sand," is to try to explain history in the context of subsequent events. True, the New Deal coalition reassembled by Truman in 1948 would fall upon hard times in the early 1950s, but even then the problems would not be permanent. Genuinely important issues and events during Truman's last four years in the White House and after brought on those hard times for the Democrats. Simply put, Truman won in 1948 by capitalizing on the natural majority enjoyed by the Democrats, the improvement of his popular image resulting from his tough stance in the escalating Cold War, and the monumental errors of Thomas Dewey as a campaigner. Even the splintering off of the two extremist factions from his party proved helpful, since they repelled many disgruntled voters back toward the center of the Democratic party, and thus to Truman.

Among the forces of continuity from the New Deal coalition in Truman's victory were organized labor, farmers, and blacks. Labor strongly backed the president in reaction to the Republican-sponsored Taft-Hartley Act and because Truman effectively used the theme that the GOP, by killing OPA, was responsible for inflation. Farmers—especially in the Midwest—switched to Truman in large numbers late in the campaign, at least partly due to a precipitous decline in corn prices by early fall, but also because of their frustration with the muddled Hope-Aiken Farm bill passed by the Eightieth Congress.

Black support for Truman was clearly explainable. By bolting the party, the Dixiecrats had instantly conferred on Truman the role of defender of black civil rights, despite the fact that the Humphrey forces at the convention had to force the administration to embrace its own civil rights proposals in the platform. In the election, the president held most of the South anyway (Thurmond won only four states), while enjoying large gains among black voters. In some key states won by Truman—California and Illinois, for example—a case could easily be made that black votes had produced the Democratic victory. Wallace, who had been thought to have strong appeal for blacks, received less than 10 percent of their votes. The pro-Truman activities of both big-city Democratic machines and labor unions undoubtedly helped to keep black voters loyal to the party. Dewey helped also, alienating black voters by soliciting votes in the white South. But finally, the president's own underdog campaign, his open courting of the black vote, and his vilification by southern segregationists enhanced the appeal of the Democratic ticket for blacks. A part of the New Deal coalition since 1936, blacks made a massive migration toward the Democrats in party identification in 1948. Four years earlier, American Institute of Public Opinion figures showed that 40 percent of black voters identified as Democrats and 40 percent as Republicans; in 1948 those figures shifted to 56 percent and 25 percent, respectively. This overwhelming Democratic loyalty among blacks would hold for at least the next four decades.

The "Communist issue" was also an asset to Truman in 1948. Though communism had posed problems for the administration a year earlier, Truman was able to preempt the issue through his handling of the Cold War in the spring and summer months, and because Henry Wallace served as a lightning rod to attract strong anti-Communist critics. Some Republicans wanted Dewey to use the issue in the campaign anyway. "The record of the administration is completely vulnerable and should be attacked," young California Congressman Richard M. Nixon advised the GOP standard bearer in September. But Dewey was determined not to be inflammatory, and treated the issue with greater temperance than even many moderates in his party. This reflected not only the governor's personal inclinations, but also, perhaps, his view that use of the issue in the 1944 race against Roosevelt had backfired. Truman, on the other hand, was less restrained, charging that "the Republicans have impeded . . . our efforts to cope with communism in this country. . . . [and have] recklessly cast a cloud of suspicion over the most loyal civil service in the world. . . . [T]hey have not hurt the Communist party one bit. They have helped it." Truman won the round in 1948, though he was to fare poorly in the larger fight looming ahead.

Finally, the president received substantial support in 1948 from Jewish voters, again despite negative omens in the months before the campaign. Faced with the problem of whether to support the partitioning of Palestine for a Jewish homeland in 1947 and early 1948, Truman wavered. In March 1948 he abandoned the concept of partition and called instead for a temporary United Nations trusteeship in Palestine. Jews and many other liberals in the United States were outraged. In May, the administration reversed its position and granted de facto recognition to the new state of Israel; by September, Truman favored extending aid to Israel and talked in terms of de jure recognition for the new nation. On election day, Jewish voters gave the president 72 percent of their votes, a healthy percentage, even if less than they had given FDR.

"I do not feel elated at the victory," President Truman said the morning after the election. "I feel overwhelmed with responsibility." The tone of humility was much the same as he had struck when he was thrust into the presidency in April 1945. This time, however, he had fought for the office and won it. It was understandable, therefore, for him to harbor hopes of moving forward with his liberal program over the next four years. Some of his liberal supporters were even more optimistic in their reading of the 1948 mandate: "Nothing less than a new era of reform has been demanded by America," exulted the liberal columnist "TRB" in the *New Republic,* "and nothing less will Americans accept."

The election had produced no such liberal mandate, as events would all too soon demonstrate. Still, the outcome had important political repercussions. As sometimes happens, a single election year had produced a new generation of bright young figures in the Democratic party, including newly elected governors Chester Bowles (Connecticut), G. Mennen Williams (Michigan), and Adlai E. Stevenson (Illinois) and Senate freshmen Paul Douglas (Illinois), Hubert Humphrey (Minnesota), Lyndon B. Johnson (Texas), and Estes Kefauver (Tennessee). As their party suffered its fourth consecutive defeat in a presidential election, many Republicans drew the moral that cooperation with the Democrats—a "me too" approach, as conservatives called it—was unwise. The future of bipartisanship in foreign policy did not look bright.

To the extent that Truman had placed highest priority on his Cold War measures and on winning the election, he had been very successful through 1948. Despite a rocky start, he appeared to have found his political footing and, though his party had seemed on the verge of fatal schism, it had in a way purified itself through the defection of Henry Wallace and his followers. Although the Dixiecrat revolt had not been averted, events of 1947 and 1948 permitted the president to put his own stamp on his party, moving it, in Irwin Ross's words, "several degrees to the left, both rhetorically and programmatically."

Yet the sky was not cloudless. With black voters holding out great hopes for administration action in their behalf, civil rights loomed as a complex, potentially explosive issue. The Republicans, consigned once again to minority status in Congress, could no longer be counted on to moderate their hostilities to the Truman administration in anticipation of an imminent accession to power. In fact, frustrated by long years out of power, they were likely to behave intractably. Nor, for all Truman's apparent foreign policy successes, was the Cold

War even close to being under control; for example, the administration had yet to define a policy in China, where a bloody civil war raged between Communists and non-Communists. Over all there remained the specter of the Communist threat at home—that issue on which Richard Nixon and others had sensed the administration to be vulnerable in 1948. Although newly elected, more popular than ever, and enjoying Democratic majorities in both houses of Congress, Harry S. Truman was in deep political trouble.

CHAPTER TWO

The Era of Hard Feelings, 1949–1952

Having been buffeted by the media, the voters, and even his own party leaders through much of his first three-plus years in the White House, the president felt vindicated by his election. "More than anything else," wrote *Newsweek,* "the election . . . convinced Harry S. Truman that Harry S. Truman was usually right." Truman's troops rallied around him almost immediately. Within the Democratic party, the liberal wing was ascendant. The ADA drew up ambitious plans for conferences and legislation, and its chairman, newly elected Senator Hubert Humphrey, symbolized the group's new focus on youth and the future. Humphrey soon had to resign his ADA office due to his Senate duties, and the group's treasury was to prove woefully inadequate to its ambitions, but in the days after Truman's election, all things seemed possible to organized liberalism.

The president signaled his intention to take the offensive with the new Congress, issuing a call from Key West, where he was vacationing, for a "reappraisal" of the State of the

Union. Virtually every major executive agency set to work to produce contributions for the annual message. Liberal advisers who had helped shape ambitious domestic proposals championed by the president in 1947 and 1948 again played key roles—such insiders as aides Clark Clifford and Charles Murphy, economist Leon Keyserling, Federal Security Administrator Oscar Ewing, and Secretary of Agriculture Charles Brannan.

Frustration of the Fair Deal

The State of the Union message, delivered on January 15, 1949, was a blockbuster. Truman renewed all the major domestic proposals from his 1945 wish list, providing a name for his program by stating that "every segment of our population and every individual has a right to expect from our Government a fair deal." Two days later, his annual economic report to the Congress fleshed out the Fair Deal program. Particularly attractive to party liberals was a proposed industrial growth policy; going beyond the parameters of the Employment Act of 1946, the plan was to give the president authority to increase plant facilities in "basic" industries, such as steel. This proposal was "probably more significant for the future of our country," exulted the *New Republic,* "than any message since Roosevelt proposed the TVA."

The area of civil rights served as a litmus test for congressional attitudes; early returns were mixed, but on the whole not especially encouraging for the president. In the new Congress, Democratic House leaders pleased Truman by pushing through a measure bound to make life more difficult for the conservative coalition. The "twenty-one day rule," passed by a vote of 176 to 48 (with about half of all southern Democrats supporting it), made it possible for legislators to circumvent the conservative-dominated House Rules Committee and take a bill directly to the floor if it was reported favorably by another committee but not acted on by Rules within three weeks. In the Senate, however, Dixie-Republican lines held firm, as the conservatives blocked an effort by liberals to change the rules to make it easier to cut off filibusters designed to lengthen debate.

The outlook for civil rights legislation in the Eighty-first Congress was therefore not especially promising, despite the Democratic victory in 1948 and the relatively weak showing of Dixiecrat presidential candidate Strom Thurmond. Scott Lucas, the downstate Illinois senator who became Senate majority leader with the Democrats' victory, was a man "whose postures were liberal," but, as columnists Rowland Evans and Robert Novak put it, his "visceral instincts often tended to be conservative." In the lower house, powerful Speaker Sam Rayburn, who hailed from rural Texas, was unenthusiastic about passing new civil rights laws. Southerners in both houses became even more organized, holding separate caucuses of their own, and their leader, Senator Richard Russell of Georgia, was accorded equal treatment by the media with the Democratic and Republican leaders.

Predictably, Truman's civil rights proposals got nowhere. By 1950, all that had been produced was a very weak FEPC bill passed by the House, as the president agreed to delay the issue in the Senate in order to get action on his foreign aid requests. Truman, therefore, settled for what he could accomplish by executive action. In October 1949, he nominated a black, William R. Hastie, as circuit court judge, the highest judicial post yet to be held by one of his race. Two months later, the Federal Housing Administration announced it would bar federal assistance in the financing of property where occupancy was restricted on the basis of race, creed, or color. In addition, the Justice Department, as it had done earlier, filed briefs supporting desegregation in cases concerning education and interstate commerce. In May 1950, the President's Committee on Equality of Treatment and Opportunity in the Armed Forces (the Fahy Committee), following up Truman's executive order of two years earlier, reported that segregation had been formally abolished in the services (though the practice continued to exist in pockets until undermined by the exigencies of war in Korea).

By early 1950, Truman was back in a familiar position on civil rights: distrusted—and to a degree held captive—by southerners, yet suspected of selling out by liberals and blacks. As the rest of the Fair Deal ran onto rocky shoals and as foreign policy became more pressing, he was forced to make tactical choices that further reduced the already slim possibilities for action on civil rights.

As early as February 1949, the president vented his wrath publicly at the obstructionism of a Congress his party supposedly controlled, declaring in a Jefferson-Jackson Day speech that "[t]he special interests are fighting us just as if they had never heard of November the 2nd. . . . They are again trying to frighten the people with the old worn out bugaboo that socialism is taking over Washington." On issue after issue, the White House was thwarted. The president's proposed comprehensive health care program, including a plan for national health insurance, was vigorously opposed by the American Medical Association as "socialized medicine," and never made it to the floor of either house; funds for hospital construction were all that Congress would approve. An ambitious public housing proposal, endorsed in modified form by Senator Taft, was passed over opposition from the real estate lobby, but the ensuing authorization for construction funds fell far short of the original administration goal. Truman met with even less success in his effort to get federal aid for education, as issues of race and religion scuttled the plan.

Another cause important to the president was repeal of the Taft-Hartley Act, a frequent theme in his 1948 campaign. On this issue opposition to the White House was formidable. *Congressional Digest* noted that more than 70 percent of the senators and congressmen who had voted to override Truman's veto of the law in 1947 had been returned to their seats in 1948. Moreover, as a *New York Times* reporter wrote, "[t]he vote on the Taft-Hartley repeal is . . . the payoff the Republicans will exact for the assistance G.O.P. Senators gave the

Dixiecrats in the civil rights fight." After several strikes, including another walkout by John L. Lewis's United Mine Workers, further damaged chances for repeal, Truman finally beat a tactical retreat. In late 1949, he unveiled a new approach, dismissing the importance of Taft-Hartley altogether and arguing that the "implied powers" of the presidency were sufficient to cope with any excesses on the part of labor unions.

In two other major areas, resource policy and agriculture, Truman also encountered frustration in 1949 and 1950. His proposed Columbia Valley Administration, modeled on TVA and intended as the first of several comprehensive power development plans, was blocked, and opposition from the powerful oil and natural gas industry blocked the nomination of the relatively consumer-oriented Leland Olds for a second term as chairman of the Federal Power Commission. Truman enjoyed a measure of revenge in the spring of 1950, however, when he successfully vetoed a bill that would have exempted natural gas producers from regulation of the prices they charged to pipelines.

In agriculture, the centerpiece of administration policy was the Brannan Plan, named for the secretary of agriculture who was its architect. Essentially a measure to provide a guaranteed income to farmers while allowing commodity prices to find their own level in the open market, the Brannan Plan struck many critics as socialistic. It was also opposed by labor, which thought farmers should not be specially favored with guaranteed incomes. The Brannan Plan was defeated in the House in July 1949, and never reached the Senate floor.

"Trying to make the 81st Congress perform is and has been worse than cussing the 80th," confided Truman to his diary in late 1949. "There are some terrible chairmen in the 81st. . . . I've kissed more S.O.B. so-called Democrats and left-wing Republicans than all the Presidents put together. I have very few people fighting my battles in Congress as I fought F.D.R.'s." Yet the president, in blaming the "terrible" leaders and S.O.B.s, failed to see the whole picture. As both Hamby (*Beyond the New Deal*) and Donald McCoy (*The Presidency of Harry S. Truman*) have pointed out, blockage of Fair Deal proposals in 1949–1950 accurately reflected the public temper. Concludes McCoy: "Truman's Fair Deal had little chance of being enacted, for the deck was stacked against it. Faced with the lack of a solid liberal consensus among the public and members of Congress, the president set out to accomplish too much."

The End of Bipartisanship

Bitter partisan conflict also erupted over foreign policy in 1949 and 1950. Despite the brief truce in the presidential campaign, the vaunted bipartisanship surrounding the Truman Doctrine, the Marshall Plan, and the North Atlantic Treaty had eroded during 1948. In fact, bipartisanship had been only fleeting and partial, at best. Truman had not consulted with opposition leaders as frequently as was sometimes purported, nor had such consultations much affected the shape of administration policy. Vandenberg, recipient of public accolades as the leader of "internationalist" Republicans cooperating with the White House, was roundly resented by many influential GOP legislators, including Taft and Senate Floor Leader Kenneth Wherry (Nebraska), who themselves commanded substantial followings. In January 1949, administration forces increased the likelihood of Republican noncooperation by enlarging their majority on the powerful Senate Foreign Relations Committee. What this move gained in terms of efficiency was more than balanced by GOP resentment.

Truman realized he confronted a dangerous world in 1949. Underscoring that fact was a paper prepared by the National Security Council the preceding November predicting that the Soviets had "the capability of overrunning in about 6 months all of continental Europe and the Near East as far as Cairo," and that by 1955 they could be capable of launching atomic, biological, and chemical weapons against the United States. The problem was compounded by public opinion; as John Gaddis has pointed out, a conciliatory policy toward the Soviets would be regarded "either as a sign of a 'thaw' in the Cold War, in which case support for needed defense and foreign aid programs would dry up, or as evidence of appeasement." According to Alan Harper (*The Politics of Loyalty*), the "American public simply could not stand the stress of living in the postwar world." Truman's replacement of the ailing but much-admired Secretary of State George C. Marshall with the more partisan Dean Acheson in 1949 did not help to increase public support for administration policies.

In 1949, Truman attempted a new initiative in foreign policy, calling in his inaugural address for a program of economic and technical aid for underdeveloped nations—a bold venture dubbed "Point Four" because of its position in the president's programmatic wish list. Truman asked for $45 million from Congress to launch the Point Four program; no appropriation was approved for it, however, until 1950. As part of the Foreign Economic Assistance Act of 1950, Point Four established as a goal of national policy the economic development of underdeveloped countries.

Truman also announced in his inaugural address that he would sign the North Atlantic Treaty, which he did on April 4, 1949. Whereas bipartisan cooperation had marked the early stages of negotiating the treaty, discord marked congressional action both on ratification and on the subsequent administration request for arms assistance to treaty nations. After rancorous debate, the Senate ratified the treaty on July 21, 1949, by a vote of 82 to 13; Taft was among the small but vociferous band of opponents, all Republicans. The ratification debate had been largely dominated by doubts and objections concerning military assistance to which the treaty would commit the United States, an issue that arose again when the administration presented its request to implement the treaty. Truman had to withdraw his original $1.1 billion arms request and substitute one much more limited in its grant of presidential discretion before the Republicans would support it. "We have killed the 'war lord bill,'" wrote Vandenberg to Walter Lippmann after the White House capitulated and rewrote its bill, "which could have made the President the top military dictator of all time."

More divisive was the China issue. In late 1948, Vandenberg had charged that policies concerning China "never were, and are not now, any part of the bipartisan liaison." Disappointed by their losses in the 1948 elections, Republicans jumped on Truman for the deteriorating position of Chiang Kai-shek's Nationalist forces in the Chinese civil war. The administration was vulnerable on the issue; Truman, under pressure from the so-called China bloc in Congress, had consented to include military as well as economic assistance in the China Aid Act of 1948, but by mid-1949 he still had not spent the appropriated funds.

Truman and Acheson were kept on the defensive throughout late 1949. In August, the State Department released a China *White Paper,* designed, as the president said, "to insure that our policy toward China, and the Far East as a whole, shall be based on informed and intelligent public opinion," but in fact aimed at exonerating the administration from blame for Chiang's fate in the civil war. Republicans were unimpressed. California's Senator Knowland secured approval by the Foreign Relations Committee of a resolution inviting General Douglas MacArthur to testify on the Far East situation. Meanwhile, various proposals for increased aid to Chiang were pushed by members of the China bloc in both houses.

Partisan motives surfaced with increasing frequency in the debate over China policy. In late August, Democrat Mike Mansfield of Montana introduced a measure in the House calling for investigation of the so-called China Lobby, an organized pressure group with ties to the GOP but relatively mysterious in its composition. Mansfield charged that money earlier earmarked "to help China, but siphoned off for private use, is being used to finance attacks on our Secretary of State and other officials." The investigation, however, was not undertaken. The following month, the president's nomination of W. Walton Butterworth, a State Department China specialist, to be assistant secretary of state for Far Eastern affairs brought a torrent of Republican criticism; the final vote for Butterworth's confirmation was 49–27, with Democrats voting for him by 44–0 and Republicans dividing 5 for, 27 against.

As Chiang's forces were driven from the mainland in the last month of 1949, party lines hardened in the United States. On January 5, 1950, Truman announced that no further "military aid or advice" would be provided to Chiang on Formosa, and a week later Acheson delivered his famous "defensive perimeter" speech before the National Press Club—an address intended primarily as a defense of American policies in China, but which also defined large parts of the globe (including Korea and China) as being outside the sphere of American responsibility. At a party caucus on January 17, Senate Democrats recorded their support for Truman's policy of "nonintervention" in China. In turn, Republicans stressed the need to defend Formosa, with Taft and former President Herbert Hoover delivering major addresses on the subject. Senator Styles Bridges pressed for a vote censuring the administration, while Knowland renewed an earlier campaign for Acheson's resignation. Not long after, Senator Joseph McCarthy of Wisconsin linked the China issue with that of internal security, as he began his damaging vendetta against "known Communists" in the State Department.

Events in China, as Cabell Phillips has noted (*The Truman Succession*), "gave Republican and other critics of the Truman administration their one secure hand-hold on a foreign policy issue." It permitted a line of attack, moreover, that echoed past Republican policies. "[F]rom the halcyon days of William McKinley and Manila Bay," notes Richard Fried in *Men Against McCarthy,* "the GOP had held to a more Pacific- and China-oriented set of priorities in foreign policy." For Truman, the China question not only threatened the United States position in the Cold War, but also posed strong political danger. "Nationalist defeat," Robert Donovan asserts in his recent study of the Truman presidency (*Tumultuous Years: The Presidency of Harry S. Truman, 1949–1953*), "would have been a threat for Truman's leadership if for no other reason than that it would tighten the bonds among his potential enemies: Republicans, the right-wing press, MacArthur, [*Time-Life* publisher] Henry R. Luce . . . , and the 'China lobby.' "

While partisanship intensified over events in China, another equally disturbing event occurred: detonation by the Soviets of their first atomic bomb in September 1949—about five years in advance of United States intelligence estimates. At one blow, the Russians ended the American nuclear monopoly and called into question the credibility of the fledgling Central Intelligence Agency. Truman immediately ordered a reappraisal of American atomic policy; on October 19, he approved rapid expansion of the nation's atomic energy program, including assessment of the possibilities for developing a hydrogen bomb, to be conducted by a special six-member advisory committee of the Atomic Energy Commission. When that committee later advised against a crash program to build the H-bomb, Truman turned to a second committee, consisting of Acheson, Secretary of Defense Louis Johnson, and AEC head David Lilienthal. "The outcome," in Donovan's words, "was hardly in doubt." On January 31, 1950, the White House announced that the AEC had been ordered to "continue its work on all forms of atomic weapons including the so-called hydrogen or superbomb."

Through 1949, Truman made every effort to keep defense spending low. National defense outlays totaled $11.9 billion for fiscal year 1949 and the president requested only $12.3 billion for the Pentagon for fiscal 1950. The original plan was to request even less for fiscal 1951, but events abroad called these plans into question. On the same day as the White House announcement on the hydrogen bomb, Truman established an ad hoc State-Defense Committee to reassess American defense policy; its findings were to be presented to the National Security Council in the spring of 1950. The resulting document, NSC-68, called for a total reversal of existing policy—especially the underlying premise that defense spending should be subject to domestic budgetary considerations. "[W]ithin the next four or five years," NSC-68 stated, "the Soviet Union will possess the military capability of delivering a surprise atomic attack of such weight that the United States must have substantially increased general air, ground, and sea strength, atomic capabilities, and air and civilian defenses to deter war.... [T]his contingency requires the intensification of our efforts in the fields of intelligence and research and development." The sixty-six page document, made public only in 1975, presented the specific strategies that should be followed, and concluded: "It is imperative that [the] present trend be reversed by a much more rapid and concerted build-up of the actual strength of both the United States and the other nations of the free world.... [T]his will be costly and will involve significant domestic financial and economic adjustments." The document was approved as policy by the president in September 1950.

In a way, as John Gaddis has argued in *Strategies of Containment,* formal White House approval of the document was not the critical issue, for "it was only the details of NSC-68 that were sensitive; its principal conclusions were widely publicized. ... The whole point of the document had been to shake the bureaucracy, Congress, and the general public into supporting more vigorous action." Accordingly, serious questions began to be raised by leading Republicans, particularly "unilateralists" such as Taft and former President Hoover, who feared the implications of the emerging policy—both the potential costs of becoming the "champion of the free world," and the loss of initiative implicit in such a defensive strategic posture. The North Korean invasion of South Korea in June 1950 became the catalyst for a major partisan conflict over not only these issues, but Harry S. Truman's overall conduct of American foreign policy.

The Anti-Communist Crusade

Both the hardening of administration foreign policy and the increasing stridency of Republican criticisms were related to an upsurge in anti-Communist activity in early 1950. The new "red scare" had its origins in the conviction of Alger Hiss for perjury by a U.S. District court in January. Truman's earlier "red herring" comment invited a new GOP attack; Congressman Richard Nixon wasted no time, charging in a radio address on the night of Hiss's conviction that "high officials" in the Roosevelt and Truman administrations had engaged in "definite, determined and deliberate" efforts to hide the "conspiracy" of which Hiss was part. Secretary of State Acheson worsened matters for the administration, remarking in a press conference that he would not turn away from his friend Alger Hiss. When apprised of Acheson's comment, Joseph McCarthy asked on the Senate floor whether the secretary's statement meant he would "not turn his back on any of the other Communists in the State Department." Acheson offered to resign, but Truman refused his offer.

On February 9, 1950, Joseph McCarthy delivered his soon-to-be-famous speech to the Ohio County Republican Women's Club in Wheeling, West Virginia, asserting that he held in his hand a list of known Communists in the State Department. His numbers were specific, but inconsistent. Both in answering questions about his charges at Wheeling and in a similar speech in Reno, Nevada, the next evening, McCarthy gave differing totals of "known Communists." But the numerical accuracy of his charges mattered less than the idea that such a conspiracy existed. The recentness of Hiss's conviction, combined with the apparent legitimacy of McCarthy's comments because he was a senator, kindled public suspicion immediately. When McCarthy followed up his Reno speech with a demagogic telegram to Truman, demanding that the president release to Congress confidential reports from the files of the Employee Loyalty Program, Truman exploded. Indulging in his characteristic habit of drafting uncensored messages reflecting his inner feelings, the president wrote out a reply to McCarthy that was never sent. "[T]his is the first time in my experience, and I was ten years in the Senate, that I ever heard of a Senator trying to discredit his own Government before the world," he wrote. "Your telegram . . . shows conclusively that you are not even fit to have a hand in the operation of the Government of the United States."

The climate was right for McCarthy's charges. Through its words and actions, the administration fed public paranoia about Communist subversion. The Justice Department had pressed intermittently since 1948 for more stringent internal security legislation, with Truman neither authorizing nor preventing its efforts. Various foreign policy pronouncements by Truman and Acheson had played up the Communist threat abroad; it was a simple step for the public to conclude that the threat existed at home as well. Moreover, the administration's Employee Loyalty Board had investigated thousands of federal employees, which implied the existence of fire behind the smoke. Evidence of the growing grass roots concern about domestic communism could be found not only in earlier investigations but also in the more than 300 sedition and anti-subversion laws passed by state legislatures.

McCarthy was motivated by his own anti-Communist feelings, as were other conservative Republicans. In *A Conspiracy So Immense,* David Oshinsky lays to rest the "dinner at the Colony" explanation for McCarthy's Wheeling speech, which holds that the senator was convinced by two Georgetown University faculty members and a Washington attorney to undertake his crusade. The Wisconsinite's efforts, Oshinsky contends, began well before his early 1950 dinner with them at the Colony restaurant. Like other Republicans, McCarthy had used the issue in the election campaigns of 1946 and 1948. The Russian A-bomb, the fall of China, and Hiss's conviction gave the GOP an irresistible opportunity to inflict perhaps mortal wounds.

The administration reacted to McCarthy's charges with concern. "The important question," wrote a Truman aide in an internal White House memorandum, is "[d]oes State know if McCarthy has anything the House of Representatives didn't have two years ago?" What troubled the White House most, according to Oshinsky—and perhaps what made McCarthy so believable—was the specificity of his allegations; the actual number of cases did not matter so much as the fact that he had cited a specific number. As the administration huddled to determine a counterstrategy, even McCarthy's conservative colleagues held back for a time from supporting him. "[A] perfectly reckless performance," opined Senator Taft, who would shortly embrace the Wisconsinite's arguments, if not his methods.

In the parlance of a later political crisis, Truman tried throughout the spring of 1950 to "stonewall," for the most part ignoring McCarthy. The president observed at his March 30 press conference: "The greatest asset that the Kremlin has is Senator McCarthy." At the same time, administration forces put in motion a Senate subcommittee investigation of McCarthy's charges, with veteran Maryland conservative Democrat Millard Tydings at its head. Ostensibly, the panel was to investigate the veracity of the charges; in fact, as Alan Harper has written, the Tydings committee "was to 'get' McCarthy, just as the Republican leadership judged his real job to be to 'get' the administration."

As the potential value of McCarthy's crusade became clear to Republican officeholders, they flocked to his side. Richard Nixon helped him by supplying secret information gathered by HUAC, and such prominent GOP senators as Taft and Bridges issued statements of support. But GOP leaders doubted that the erratic McCarthy was the right man for the job; judging him to be expendable, they determined to play down their support for the Wisconsin senator, while giving him background assistance.

Truman, whether or not he was yet worried, was certainly annoyed. "I am in the midst of the most terrible struggle any President ever had," he wrote his cousin. In a March press conference, he alleged that Wherry and Bridges were attempting to "sabotage" American foreign policy. The president found himself gripped in a political vice—in the sympathetic phrase of Alonzo Hamby, "between the justifiable liberal criticisms of the loyalty program and the groundless onslaughts of the hysterical anti-Communist right."

The outbreak of war in Korea diverted Truman from focusing on McCarthy, but the Tydings subcommittee ground on with its investigation through the summer of 1950, concluding with a strongly partisan report, issued in July, that its Republican members would not even sign. Highly critical of McCarthy, the report was accepted by the Senate on a straight party-line vote, after what Oshinsky labels "the meanest Senate debate in recent memory." Undaunted, McCarthy kept up his barrage, inside and outside the Senate. Aside from a "declaration of conscience" against his methods written by Maine's GOP Senator Margaret Chase Smith and signed by a handful of other moderate Republicans, the only outcry from within Congress came from proadministration forces; southerners and most GOP moderates sat silent. Meanwhile, the popularity of McCarthy and his crusade grew, as reflected in a ditty forwarded to McCarthy as an "official ballad." Titled "Fall in Line with Joe McCarthy," and sung to the tune of "The Battle Hymn of the Republic," the song captured, in its first stanza, the spirit of the anti-red crusade:

This is the land of freedom and when the Communists appear
They represent a menace we must recognize and fear.
So get behind the movement of the modern Paul Revere.
His truth is marching on.

The Korean War and American Politics

On Saturday, June 24, 1950 (U.S. time), while Harry Truman was beginning a brief vacation in Missouri, Communist North Korean troops invaded South Korea across the thirty-eighth parallel. Acheson, informed that evening, waited until Sunday morning to call Truman. By that night, the president was at Blair House in Washington, meeting with top aides. Evidence from oral histories and memoirs, according to Donovan, indicates that Truman had decided before the meeting "to fight, if necessary to hit back at the North Koreans and thwart their attack." This predisposition was consistent with Truman's decisive—some would say impulsive—approach to crises.

American occupation troops had been removed from South Korea a year earlier, in the hope that North and South would peacefully reunite. The North Korean invasion, backed, if not initiated, by the Soviets, ended that hope. Truman's first decisions were to have General MacArthur, then heading the American occupation forces in Tokyo, send military supplies to South Korea; to start the American Seventh Fleet on its way from the Philippines to the Formosa Straits; and to have the air force draw up plans for the destruction of all Soviet air bases in the Far East. The next day, he ordered the fleet into the Formosa Straits, designated substantial additional aid to the Philippines and the French in Indochina, and without hesitation committed American planes and ships to aid South Korea. Having already obtained from the U.N. Security Council a resolution branding North Korea the aggressor, on June 27 the administration won Security Council approval of a resolution calling on U.N. member nations to render assistance to South Korea. Within three days, Truman acted to meet that call, committing U.S. ground forces to what would be a bloody three-year conflict, the Korean "police action."

The president's decisive actions won quick support from the media and the public. "A clean wind moved across the nation last week," *Newsweek* editorialized. "Tired of murky defeats, inconclusive victories, and faulty diplomatic footwork, Americans were revived by Harry S. Truman's immediate counterpunch against the Communists in East Asia." In this atmosphere only the "extreme isolationist press," as James MacGregor Burns wrote in the *New York Times Magazine,* gave support to rising criticisms from congressional Republicans concerning the *way* Truman had made his decisions on Korea. A number of GOP legislators had expressed misgivings immediately, including Taft, who on June 28 railed on the Senate floor against the "complete usurpation by the President of authority to use the armed forces of the country." At a meeting of legislative leaders on June 30 before Truman announced he was sending in ground troops, Wherry combatively interrogated the chief executive as to whether a decision on ground troops would be made without further consultation with congressional leaders. He drew from the president the disingenuous response, "If there is any necessity for Congressional action, I will come to you. But I hope we can get these bandits in Korea suppressed without that."

It was probably still possible for Truman to have secured a congressional authorizing resolution for the "police action" well into July. Yet, despite the urgings of some of his advisers, he chose not to seek it. A draft resolution that circulated within the administration early in the month went nowhere. A Truman aide later explained that the congressional leaders themselves argued against requesting such a resolution, on the grounds that it might prove divisive. Truman may also have been influenced by Acheson, who opposed the tactic. In any case, the opportunity passed. There can be little doubt that the president "acted within his constitutional rights," as Donald McCoy has written. "The real question was whether it was politic for [him] not to ask for a congressional resolution."

By late summer, Truman began to pay for his decision. As the military tide turned against the U.N.–U.S. forces under the command of General MacArthur, dismayed Republicans stepped up their condemnations of the president for abusing his executive power, and revived earlier charges about the "sell out" of China. The war in Korea, they claimed, had been brought on by the administration's "betrayal" of Nationalist leader Chiang Kai-shek, who was opposing the Communists in China. McCarthyism was thus smoothly joined with opposition to the administration's conduct of the war.

From the battlefield in Korea, MacArthur abetted the administration's critics, releasing the text of a message to the Veterans of Foreign Wars national convention in August 1950 that, while nominally within the bounds of existing strategy, harshly criticized the Truman-Acheson policy toward China. "Nothing could be more fallacious," wrote the general, "than the threadbare argument by those who advocate appeasement and defeatism in the Pacific that if we defend Formosa we alienate continental Asia." Furious, Truman directed Secretary of Defense Louis Johnson to get the general to recall his statement. When Johnson, a supporter of MacArthur, balked, Truman himself had to order the general's recantation. But it was too late; the offending message appeared in *U.S. News & World Report,* publicly exposing the rift between the president and the general. Truman's dramatic trip to Wake Island in October to meet with MacArthur appeared temporarily to patch things up, but later events would prove that MacArthur, like the Republicans who championed him, was irreconcilable where the administration's handling of the war was concerned.

Lambasting the administration for unpreparedness, which they claimed had invited aggression in Korea, Republicans concentrated their fire on Acheson and Louis Johnson. Truman remained loyal to Acheson, but on September 12, he forced Johnson to resign. Johnson, though publicly associated with the defense budget cuts of the previous year, had been judged expendable by Truman because of his ambitions and insubordinate attitude. "Potomac fever and a pathological condition [were] to blame," confided the president to his diary.

Trying to blunt partisan criticism, Truman selected popular former Secretary of State General George C. Marshall to succeed Johnson at Defense, but the move failed to mollify the Republicans. Since by law no individual could be secretary of defense who had served in the armed forces during the preceding ten years, special legislative clearance was needed before Marshall could take the post. The waiver passed, but Republicans voted against it by 100 to 27 in the House, and 20 to 10 in the Senate.

Passage of the McCarran Internal Security Act in September 1950 gave further evidence that the political initiative had swung to the right. In August, Truman had tried to blunt the efforts of Republicans and conservative Democrats, led by McCarran, to revive a measure proposed earlier by then-Representatives Karl Mundt and Nixon to require Communists to register and to bar Communists and leaders of "front" organizations from holding government positions. Truman's response to the revival of the Mundt-Nixon bill was to deliver a special message to Congress boasting of the administration's internal security record and requesting moderate legislation. But in the superheated political climate, the new McCarran bill, originally directed primarily at registration and prosecution of Communists, was made far more extreme when an amendment providing for emergency internment of subversives, intended by liberal Democrats as a substitute for the entire bill, was added before passage. Truman's veto was overridden by huge margins in both houses.

Republicans were intent on making the Korean conflict an issue in the 1950 congressional elections. In August, the GOP National Committee issued a fifty-nine-page campaign document that was sharply critical of the administration. "The area of bipartisan foreign policy is clearly defined," it began. "Asia, including China and Korea, has been excluded." The document rehashed charges about Democratic failures at Yalta and in China, and concluded with a lengthy quotation from MacArthur's speech to the Veterans of Foreign Wars. GOP legislators escalated their attacks on the administration with each new twist in the war. In September, the temporary reversal of military fortunes following MacArthur's successful amphibious assault at Inchon led large numbers of administration critics to embrace the general's "all-out" strategy for victory. The subsequent surprise entry of Communist Chinese regulars into the conflict in late October, which might have dampened such criticism, only worsened the situation, as Republicans linked to the "China lobby" became even more outspoken.

"The Korean War," Richard Fried has written in *Men Against McCarthy,* "accentuated all the anxieties that came under the heading of 'communism' and altered political strategies in both parties." In the fall of 1950, GOP congressional campaigns across the country were dominated by McCarthyism and the war issue, with AMA attacks on the administration's health insurance plan, criticisms of the Brannan Plan, and rumors of administration connections with organized crime (stemming from hearings conducted by Senator

Estes Kefauver of Tennessee) playing lesser roles. Most Democratic candidates shied away from Fair Deal issues. One of the most dramatic races was the California Senate campaign in which Nixon defeated liberal Democrat Helen Gahagan Douglas. (Douglas was "pink right down to her underwear," charged Nixon, in one of his less tasteful campaign remarks.) In Maryland, McCarthy and his henchmen intervened in Millard Tydings's reelection contest and, by use of unfair tactics exposed only later, helped to defeat Tydings in retribution for his role in the committee report chastising the Wisconsinite. McCarthy also went after Democratic Senate Majority Leader Lucas in Illinois, and liberal disarmament proponent Brien McMahon, seeking reelection to the Senate from Connecticut. McMahon won, though several administration supporters—including Lucas—were less fortunate. Overall, GOP gains were smaller in 1950 than was usual for the out-party in off-year elections. The party picked up five seats in the Senate and twenty-eight in the House; the Democrats remained in control of both.

Because McCarthy and his supporters had been so visible in Republican campaigns, the media generally portrayed the results as public endorsement of McCarthyism and repudiation of the Truman-Acheson policies. "[N]o Democratic politician in the Senate or House," wrote one party insider shortly after the election, "will undertake to defend the Department of State in the next session of the Congress." In truth, it was the whole host of issues growing out of the Korean War that hurt the Democrats. "On balance," concludes Fried, " . . . the Korean War helped the Republicans; it provided a topic less to be argued than simply mentioned." White House aide George Elsey later offered the opinion that if the Democrats had counterattacked more vigorously they would have done better. This is unlikely. The very reason administration forces did not go on the offensive was that the political climate was so rough for them that it left them shell-shocked.

The Republicans and their supporters acted as if they were big winners. Shortly after the election, a suggestion came to the president that he appoint a new secretary of state and begin regular consultations with "the outstanding senators-elect." Another proposal, offered privately to the president by Republican Congressman Jacob Javits of New York, was that he name General Dwight D. Eisenhower "a sort of 'deputy president' . . . in over-all charge . . . of the mobilization effort." Truman's only response to such suggestions was to maintain a facade of bipartisan consultation, holding regular White House meetings for the leaders of both parties, even though his mind was usually made up beforehand. Unappeased, the House and Senate Republican conferences passed separate resolutions demanding that Truman dismiss Acheson—the first such calls since Congress had asked Lincoln to remove Secretary of State William Seward.

In late December 1950, the president greatly increased Republican antagonism toward administration policies by announcing he would send American troops to Europe to participate in the newly formed Western European defense command under NATO auspices. Although he had indicated three months earlier that troops might be sent in the future, the specificity and timing of his December announcement provoked the Republicans. Declining fortunes in Korea had already inflamed GOP attitudes, and the possibility of permanent American military involvement in Europe—as in Korea, by unilateral presidential action—was too much for some party members to bear. The result was a "Great Debate" over American foreign policy that lasted well into the spring.

The debate began in earnest when the Eighty-second Congress convened in January 1951. In the House, a measure was introduced to ban the use of future appropriations for sending American troops abroad unless Congress specifically approved such an action; it was swiftly referred to committee. Taft and Wherry were more successful, however, in stirring up debate in the Senate. On January 5, Taft delivered a ten-thousand-word speech that set the themes for the months that followed. "Members of Congress, and particularly members of the Senate," he asserted, "have a constitutional obligation to reexamine constantly and discuss the foreign policy of the United States." Denying that extended foreign policy debate would give "aid and comfort" to the enemy, the Ohioan railed at length against administration secrecy in the making of foreign policy; the ineffectiveness of the nation's military posture under Truman; the mistaken attempt to battle communism "on the vast land areas" of Europe and Asia (he favored greater reliance on air and sea power); and the failure to call upon Chiang Kai-shek for military aid in Korea.

Three days after Taft's speech, Wherry introduced a resolution stating that no American troops could be sent to Europe "pending determination by Congress of a policy on that matter." In the course of the long debate that ensued, most Republicans vigorously supported the Taft-Wherry position.

In February 1951, to blunt the GOP attack, Truman bought NATO commander Eisenhower home to testify before the House Armed Services and Senate Foreign Relations committees. Republican leaders were not uniformly impressed by the general's testimony, which favored virtually unlimited power for the president to commit troops to NATO's defense. Taft, in fact, made his differences with Eisenhower so clear that journalists began to speculate about a Taft-Eisenhower confrontation for the Republican nomination in 1952.

Eventually, two similar measures passed: a simple Senate resolution that would not have the force of law, and a concurrent resolution, also without statutory authority but requiring House action. Both expressed the sense of the Senate that the president might send troops "to contribute our fair share of the forces" for NATO, but provided that the chief executive should consult with Congress before actually sending troops abroad. Truman signaled his intention to ignore the latter provision, claiming that the outcome was "further evidence, that the country stands firm in support of the North Atlantic Treaty."

Meanwhile, American troops fared poorly in Korea. After the successes following Inchon, the engagement of Chinese Communist troops helped the North Koreans push the U.N.

forces southward to the thirty-eighth parallel. In December, Truman had requested additional defense funds from Congress, bringing the total to $42 billion for fiscal 1951; NSC-68, formally approved by the president in September 1950, was now settled policy. By early 1951, public opinion polls showed a frustrated ambivalence among American voters: along with strong sentiment for using the atomic bomb against the Chinese, the polls showed considerable support for withdrawing altogether from the war.

In part, of course, such ambivalence and impatience was an inevitable byproduct of "limited" war—that is, warfare conducted short of using all available force, and apparently aimed at less than total victory. This was a phenomenon new to the American experience and seemed an almost impossibly ambivalent concept. Republican criticisms of administration war policy reflected intense frustration with the "limited" war approach. Finally, with the position of the U.S. forces much improved as a result of a successful counteroffensive engineered by General Matthew Ridgway, President Truman shifted course. In late March, he informed the allied governments of his intention to seek a cease-fire in Korea.

Though General MacArthur had been informed in advance of Truman's announcement, he was unable to remain silent. In a March 20 letter to Republican House Minority Leader Joseph Martin, he denounced the administration's "no win" policy. When on April 5, Martin read the general's letter on the House floor, MacArthur's days as commander in Korea were clearly numbered. In the early morning hours of April 11, 1951, Truman summoned members of the press to the White House to announce the general's dismissal.

Congressional Republicans were outraged. "Our only choice is to impeach President Truman," Indiana McCarthyite William Jenner told the Senate the next day, "and find out who is the secret invisible government which has so cleverly led our country down the road to destruction." Impeachment was in fact considered by Republican leaders of the two houses, meeting in Martin's office the same morning. Yet they abandoned the idea, feeling, however begrudgingly, that Truman had probably not acted unconstitutionally in sacking Mac-Arthur. Instead it was decided there would be an official Senate investigation into the matter.

Public reaction to the firing was explosive. Mail on both sides of the issue flooded the White House and congressional offices (even the White House's own count showed mail to the president running heavily in favor of MacArthur). *Newsweek* reported that one Los Angeles man who supported the president had broken a radio over the head of his wife, who was a partisan of the general, as the two quarreled while listening to news of the dismissal. In New York, two thousand longshoremen walked off their jobs to protest the president's action, and demonstrations erupted throughout the country, complete with hangings of both principals in effigy.

In this atmosphere, MacArthur returned to address a joint session of the Congress on April 19. The general outdid himself. In an eloquent and melodramatic address, he defended his position, accusing the administration of defeatism, and closing with a promise to "just fade away." His fading was noisy, however, and slow to occur, as his partisans directed a barrage of criticism at Truman, and the general himself made little secret of his availability for the GOP nomination in 1952.

Meanwhile, the administration worked to shore up the president's position. Within a week of the dismissal, White House aides were drawing up questions for friendly members of the Senate to ask the cashiered general in the upcoming hearings. Plans were formulated also for a counterattack on pro-MacArthur Republicans, including possible investigation of the "China lobby." There was even a suggestion from a White House staff member to use "dirty tricks" to discredit MacArthur himself—for instance, by revealing that the famous photograph showing him wading ashore at Leyte in World War II had been a sham, done for newsreel cameras while troops were actually coming ashore on a dry pier. Wisely, this plan was not seriously pursued. As Hamby has noted, MacArthur's dismissal made Democratic unity essential to Truman, and he worked successfully to win the active support of such powerful party conservatives as Senators Richard Russell and Robert Kerr (Oklahoma). Russell's backing was particularly valuable, for he was named to chair the joint hearings on the dismissal.

The avowed objective of the Senate hearings, which began on May 3, 1951, was to inquire into the course of American policy in the Far East and particularly in the Korean War. Given the composition of the joint committee (Armed Services and Foreign Relations), the administration could hope for a sympathetic verdict. The White House strategy was to keep the hearings going, feed prepared questions to "friends" on the committee, and see that the investigation got extensive press coverage.

When the lengthy hearings ended in mid-August, the administration had clearly succeeded in its tactics. The probe led to no important change in Truman's policies, toward either Europe or Asia. Administration witnesses, such as Marshall, Acheson, and General Omar N. Bradley, proved effective. When the committee voted 20–3 on August 17 not to issue a formal report, the message was that Truman had acted within his authority and there was no basis for criticism of the conduct of the war. Russell explained that most members "felt that such an appearance of divided counsels on national foreign policy would adversely affect the current truce negotiations" in Korea, as well as negotiations then underway for a World War II peace treaty with Japan.

Historians agree that right was on the president's side in the MacArthur episode, and that the clash between the two was inevitable. The general, writes McCoy, "had been guilty of insubordination . . . and his indiscretions had helped to earn him a back seat in the efforts to turn the [Korean] conflict around since Christmas 1950. Consequently, MacArthur became more restive, knowing that he was only technically in command in the Far East." Once the conflict became unresolvable, and Truman fired his commander, important results followed. "Indubitably," concludes Donovan, the whole MacArthur drama turned people more than ever against the frustrating limited war. Indubitably, it divided public opinion on what should be done in the Far Eastern stalemate. There is little doubt that the [general's] speech strengthened the Republican party and no doubt whatever that it hurt Truman politically and weakened his leadership in the home stretch.

But if key GOP leaders, such as Taft, took heart and became more aggressive in condemning administration policies in Korea after April 1951, it was at least as significant that Truman survived the crisis.

When the administration initiated truce negotiations with the North Koreans in early July 1951, Republicans were predictably critical. Repeating his tactical error of a year earlier, Truman had not bothered to consult with appropriate congressional leaders before embarking on the peace talks. He thereby missed a chance to put the truce question before Congress and force Republicans to go on record one way or the other. "This is a very delicate matter," the president told his aides, "and if those fellows up on the Hill start making speeches they'll blow the whole thing out of the water." So the talks proceeded, sporadically, without a congressional imprimatur, and in the face of mounting U.S. casualties.

Domestic issues growing out of the Korean War also caused Truman problems in 1950 and 1951. Specifically, the administration had to combat public fears of inflation by keeping prices and wages down, while at the same time ensuring adequate production levels to support the military effort. On July 19, 1950, the president asked Congress for a moderate program of credit controls combined with government assistance for industrial expansion. Congress, eager to be rid of what it saw as a political hot potato, gave Truman much more, granting him discretionary power to impose price, wage, and rent controls. Truman went on television in mid-December to declare a state of national emergency, activating the economic powers he had been granted.

Truman used his reorganization authority to create a new Office of Defense Management (ODM) under General Electric president Charles E. Wilson. Despite a temporary rift with labor leaders, the administration was able to avert major problems with work stoppages, while inflation slowed. From spring 1951 to the end of the war, the cost-of-living index remained nearly level.

Republicans criticized the war vociferously, but not very constructively. Party spokesmen, in the words of Ronald Caridi (*The Korean War and American Politics*), were "motivated more by political expediency than by a desire to present a consistent and viable alternative to Administration policies." But the criticisms hurt; after June 1950, heightened GOP antagonism not only made conduct of the war itself politically difficult, but stymied the Fair Deal and gave added encouragement and support to Joseph McCarthy in his crusade against subversives in the Truman administration.

Truman under Siege

Truman endured a difficult final two years in the White House. The Senate, with new McCarthyite Republicans and the increased self-confidence of southern Democrats, who knew the president desperately needed their votes on defense and foreign policy, promised to be especially troublesome. As Hamby has written, Truman "had to choose between an almost certainly foredoomed attempt to build a Fair Deal majority in Congress and an effort . . . to salvage the internationalist coalition." To accomplish the latter goal, the president made no effort to win over Republicans, most of whom he had come to regard as hopeless. Rather, he actively courted conservative southerners and westerners in his own party—such as Senators Russell and Kerr—by placing the Fair Deal so far on the back burner that it was hardly visible, and yielding on certain issues of specific interest to them.

In keeping with this strategy, Truman's 1951 State of the Union address concentrated on defense and foreign policy. Aid to education, health insurance, and unemployment assistance were mentioned, but not emphasized, and civil rights and labor reform were all but ignored. The last two areas received predictably little attention from either president or Congress in the year that followed. Aside from vetoing a prosegregationist school construction bill, the president exerted no further pressure on Congress in behalf of black rights.

Truman also soft-pedaled other domestic issues. Concerning Taft-Hartley, he decided by spring 1952 to ask for a bipartisan congressional "study" of the law—which was later aborted due to the steel crisis. Similarly, the administration's crusade for national health insurance ended with a whimper, as Truman settled for appointment of a blue-ribbon study commission at the end of 1951. Its report, issued a year later, pushed for a moderate government program to help provide health care for all Americans, but no congressional action followed. Finally, the troublesome farm issue was temporarily resolved by a 1952 compromise measure that provided 90 percent-of-parity government price supports, a measure that fell far short of the sweeping reform represented by the moribund Brannan Plan. The only domestic policy area where the president acted decisively was in taxes; the Revenue Act of 1951, designed to raise $5.5 billion, provided needed revenues, even though it perpetuated a number of allowances and loopholes that Truman opposed. Most important, it allowed him to leave office with a national debt lower in real dollars than that which he had inherited in 1945.

Truman's troubles were compounded by revelations of corruption in his administration. Beginning with an investigation of the Reconstruction Finance Corporation in early 1951, conducted by a Senate subcommittee chaired by Senator J. W. Fulbright (whom Truman characterized afterwards as "an overeducated s.o.b."), the president was buffeted by attacks on the integrity of his aides and associates. Tales abounded of "five percenters" and those who took gifts, such as freezers and mink coats, for "assistance" in securing contracts and government favors for individuals willing and able to pay. Included among the alleged "five percenters" was Harry Vaughan, the president's military aide and close friend. Most damaging to the administration's reputation were televised hearings conducted by Democratic Senator Estes Kefauver of Tennessee. The Kefauver Committee, which began by focusing on gambling, turned up links between Democratic party leaders and organized crime figures. Senator Kefauver profited from the televised probe. As the press mentioned the Tennessean more and more frequently as a presidential or vice presidential possibility for 1952, Truman grew increasingly resentful of him.

The leading historian of the Kefauver crime hearings parallels Truman's handling of the crime issue with his approach to anti-Communist activities. "As the . . . administration had attempted to contain and direct the 'red menace' with its rhetoric and loyalty programs," writes William Moore in *The Kefauver Committee and the Politics of Crime, 1950–1952,* "it also tried to ride out the hysteria over crime with modest bureaucratic directives and fumbling motions at cooperation with state and municipal officials." The Kefauver Committee finished its work in September 1951, but charges of wrongdoing continued to plague the administration—specifically, allegations of rampant corruption in the Internal Revenue Service. Eventually, after being forced to sacrifice a special investigator he had drawn from the private sector, Truman replaced Attorney General J. Howard McGrath with former Congressman and Circuit Judge James P. McGranery, who turned out to be a great improvement. Attacks on the integrity of the administration continued, however, and the issue of corruption was a major theme of the GOP's 1952 campaign.

McCarthyism also intensified in the last two years of Truman's presidency, reinforced by the seeming endlessness of the Korean involvement. Attempting to regain the initiative from his critics, in January 1951 the president announced the appointment of a special Commission on Internal Security and Individual Rights, to be chaired by Admiral Chester W. Nimitz. The so-called Nimitz Commission never went to work, however, as the Senate refused to approve the usual waiver of conflict-of-interest status for its members. In October 1951,

Truman accepted the resignations of all commission members including Nimitz, and he did not attempt to revive the body. Athan Theoharis has argued in *Seeds of Repression* that Republican congressional opposition to the Nimitz Commission was "well-founded," because through it Truman was unwisely seeking to by-pass Congress and "to establish the administration's absolute expertise in loyalty matters." If the president erred in trying this end run, however, his critics were guilty of narrow and partisan motives. Ultimately, as Hamby has concluded, the commission was derailed by McCarthyites who feared that it "would take the Communist issue out of politics."

Truman never really discovered how to combat McCarthyism. In April 1951, he accelerated the anti-Communist witch hunt by allowing the Loyalty Review Board to change its grounds for dismissal of employees from "reasonable grounds . . . for belief that the person involved is disloyal" to "reasonable doubt" about the person's loyalty. Yet four months later, in the face of an ongoing assault by McCarthy against the State Department (including a brutal attack on Marshall), Truman denounced the senator and his methods in the harshest terms. "We want to protect the country against disloyalty—of course we do . . . ," the president said before the American Legion on August 14, 1951. "But we don't want to destroy our whole system of justice in the process. . . . [T]he scurrilous work of the scandalmongers gravely threatens the whole idea of protection for the innocent in our country today."

A small band of Senate Democrats, led by William Benton of Connecticut, tried to bring about McCarthy's expulsion from the upper house, but to no avail. Extensive hearings into the Wisconsinite's involvement in the 1950 Maryland Senate campaign yielded evidence of wrongdoing but produced no action against him. Meanwhile, the president flailed futilely against his strident anti-Communist critics, weakened by his own irresolute policies as well as by GOP perceptions that his powers were slipping. Like corruption, the issue of Communists in government remained a strong weapon against Truman and the Democrats into the 1952 election campaign.

Yet another crisis emerged in spring 1952, as labor-management conflict arose to plague Truman once again. On the last day of 1951, labor contracts with the steel industry expired; an impasse soon developed over the terms for a new agreement. Truman could have invoked the Taft-Hartley Act, appointing a fact-finding board and initiating an eighty-day "cooling off" period to postpone a possible strike. Instead, he let the Wage Stabilization Board (WSB) determine what would be a fair settlement, believing with union leaders that the steel companies were in a position to absorb a reasonable wage hike. The companies disagreed, however, and when the WSB recommended in mid-March a package of wage and fringe benefit increases, management countered with the demand that steel prices be permitted to rise accordingly. Truman firmly backed the WSB, but ODM chief Charles Wilson undermined him by publicly expressing disagreement and siding with the steel companies.

By the end of March, Wilson was gone, but the impasse remained. The companies made a final compromise offer, which was rejected by the union, and the long-feared strike was announced for 12:01 AM, April 9. Determined not to permit a work stoppage in an industry vital to the military effort in Korea, the president acted decisively. On April 8, he seized control of the steel industry on the basis of his inherent powers as commander in chief. The next morning, in a special message to Congress, he invited legislative action. Without such action, he said, he would keep the steel mills under government control until a settlement could be reached.

In the heavily politicized climate of 1952—with the Korean conflict stalemated, charges of corruption swirling about the administration, McCarthyism in full swing, and the presidential primaries underway—reaction to the steel seizure was predictable. Republicans expressed outrage at such presidential usurpation of power, while only a handful of Democrats came to Truman's defense. No fewer than four congressional investigations were launched. The press was nearly as critical as the political opposition; among major dailies, only the New York *Post* supported Truman. "Truman Does a Hitler," trumpeted the New York *Daily News.*

"The inherent powers authority had one overriding difficulty," Maeva Marcus has concluded in *Truman and the Steel Seizure Case,* "its uncertain legal basis. . . . [T]he courts had never ruled on the legality of [earlier] seizures." Some believed that the judiciary would not intervene this time either. But within a month, District Court Judge David Pine issued an injunction against the seizure. On June 2, 1952, the Supreme Court decided by six to three (Truman appointees Sherman Minton, Stanley Reed, and Fred Vinson dissenting) that Pine was right, declaring the president's action unconstitutional. The steel strike resumed when control of the mills passed back to the companies on June 3. With Congress continuing to resist Truman's urgings for legislative action to end it, the stoppage lasted fifty-three days. The final settlement, reached on July 24, differed very little from the terms suggested by the government in the spring.

"The steel seizure," Marcus notes, "provided the country with a unique opportunity for reassessing, in the aftermath of two decades of unprecedented employment of executive power, the balance of authority among the branches." Its resolution reaffirmed the existence of limits on presidential activism, but it was the courts rather than Congress that set them. Increasingly restive with Truman's conduct of the war, his handling of domestic communism, and now his unwarranted intrusion into the economy, the legislative branch—and specifically its GOP membership—was a highly frustrated junior partner in Washington.

The Election of 1952

Harry S. Truman confided to his diary on April 16, 1950, that he was "not a candidate for nomination" in 1952. Yet, as late as mid-March, 1952, Truman's top political adviser, Clark Clifford, speculated as to whether his chief would in fact be a candidate for reelection. Finally, on March 29, Truman ended all conjecture, publicly announcing his decision not to run.

It is not hard to understand the president's decision. The three issues of Korea, communism, and corruption (which a GOP senator abbreviated "K_1C_2" later in the campaign) had clearly undermined his popularity, as well as his authority. Moreover, the North-South breach in the Democratic party remained unhealed from 1948. Truman had been in the White House for nearly seven years; while he was exempted from the two-term limitation imposed by the newly ratified (in 1951) Twenty-second Amendment, the tribulations of those years surely had predisposed him to turn the reins over to a successor.

But where was that successor to be found? Truman had tried to recruit Chief Justice Fred Vinson and then, if later reports can be believed, General Dwight Eisenhower, to carry the Democratic party standard in 1952. Neither was interested—Eisenhower for reasons that became quite obvious when he publicly disclosed his preference for the Republican party. When in early 1952 the president tried to interest Illinois Governor Adlai Stevenson, a man apparently acceptable to both Fair Dealers and moderate southerners, he was again rebuffed.

Perhaps because he was frustrated in his search for a successor, Truman allowed his name to be entered in the New Hampshire primary in February. It was after losing embarrassingly to Kefauver (whom he privately judged a "demagogue dumbbell"), that he announced his withdrawal from the race. This left the contest open. Kefauver, though not without support, had substantial liabilities; he was generally regarded as a lightweight in the Senate and was reputed to have a drinking problem. The South backed Richard Russell, but the Georgian—to use Truman's phrase—was "poison to Northern Democrats and honest Liberals." Vice President Alben Barkley, who desperately wanted to run, was at seventy-four considered to be too old; Averell Harriman, judged by Truman "the ablest of them all," was interested, but lacked support outside the

Northeast. The ambitious Kefauver breezed to victory in several early primaries until he was bested by Russell in Florida, where civil rights again emerged as a divisive party issue. Meanwhile, Truman formally endorsed Stevenson, who proceeded to irritate the president by maintaining a coy demeanor until the convention itself. By that time, Truman had switched to Harriman, but it was too late. Stevenson, whose convention welcoming speech greatly impressed the delegates, was nominated on the third ballot, with the president's supporters eventually once again in his corner. To try to hold the South, the governor selected Alabama Senator John Sparkman as his running mate.

On the Republican side, the early front runner for the nomination was Taft, who—believing the Deweyites had stolen (and wasted) a nomination that had been rightfully his in 1948—confidently declared his candidacy in October 1951. His campaign, the Ohioan told the assembled press, would extol "liberty rather than the principles of socialism." Amid rumors of a possible Eisenhower candidacy, however, the polls were disquieting for Taft; even residents of his hometown Cincinnati who had voted for him for senator in 1950 preferred Eisenhower at the head of the GOP ticket. Still, on New Year's Day 1952, Taft wrote to a friend that he could not "quite see how Eisenhower is going to cut in to any substantial extent on the 600 or so delegates who are clearly favorable to me at the moment."

In the end, Taft's prediction was not far off. He came very close to winning the 604 convention votes needed to be nominated. But the moderate forces in the GOP angling for General Eisenhower's nomination, led by Senator Henry Cabot Lodge of Massachusetts and Governors James Duff of Pennsylvania and Sherman Adams of New Hampshire, built well. They engineered a 50 percent victory for the general over Taft's 38 percent in the important New Hampshire primary. The two sides battled to a near draw through the remaining primaries, with Eisenhower resigning his NATO command and returning home in early June to take control of his own destiny. The right wing's campaign against Ike was not pretty. Taft operatives in New Hampshire, for example, labeled the general a "drinking companion" of Soviet Marshal Zhukov, circulated stories of Mamie Eisenhower's alleged alcoholism, and alternately spread rumors that Ike was Jewish and that the pope had baptized him. But the Eisenhower camp outdid the Taftites when it counted, winning the crucial disputed credentials fights at the convention by means of a deceptive ploy ironically labeled the "fair play amendment." The final roll call on the first ballot at the Chicago convention was Eisenhower 845, Taft 280, but the vote had been very much closer before a series of last-minute shifts to the victor. Eager to establish credibility with the disappointed GOP right, Ike's managers convinced him to accept the thirty-eight-year-old Richard Nixon for the second spot on the ticket.

It took until September for reconciliation to occur between Eisenhower and Taft. At a conference held in New York City at the residence Eisenhower had occupied when he was president of Columbia University, the two leaders reached an accord whereby the candidate assured Taft he would support the basic principles of the Taft-Hartley Act, flexible farm price supports, and specific reductions in federal spending. Following the meeting, Taft reported that the general had embraced the fundamental issue of "liberty against creeping socialism in every domestic field."

The 1952 campaign was as bitter as it would have been if Truman and Taft had been the nominees. The Ohio senator, in fact, campaigned for Eisenhower in twenty midwestern and western states in the closing weeks of the campaign, and Truman, though privately resentful that Stevenson took pains to distance himself from the administration (even referring in print to "the mess in Washington"), could not resist active campaigning either. The president's whistle-stop tour for the Democratic ticket, rivaling his "give 'em hell" campaign of four years earlier, was of questionable value to Stevenson. "Truman's intensely partisan campaign," observes Athan

Theoharis, "enabled Eisenhower and the Republicans to assume the stance of disinterested patriots."

Personalities played an important part in the 1952 campaign—particularly General Eisenhower's heroic image—but the
issues between the two parties emerged sharply. The "K_1C_2"
formula was predictably useful to the GOP. The Republican
platform took a strongly anti-Communist line, and Eisenhower
himself—though certainly no fan of McCarthy's—seemed symbolically to join the red baiters by his controversial decision
to drop from a speech in Wisconsin a planned defense of his
mentor, General Marshall (who had been viciously denounced
by McCarthy). "Without the Marshall paragraph for balance,"
writes Oshinsky, Eisenhower's speech "sounded like an endorsement of McCarthy's crusade." The general was faulted
by moderates for caving in to McCarthyism, but the anti-Communist theme nonetheless put the Democrats on the defensive.
Stevenson and his supporters sought to disassociate themselves from more liberal groups, such as ADA, while vice presidential candidate Sparkman called attention to Eisenhower's
presidency of Columbia University—an institution, he said,
that had produced "more Communists ... than any other
school in the United States."

Korea provided an equally useful issue for the GOP. Eisenhower avoided denunciations of American involvement in
the conflict, focusing instead on the bungling policies that had
led to it. Other Republicans spoke with less restraint, such as
the Virginia House candidate who equated Democratic policies with "red-coddling, red ink, and the red blood of fighting
men."

Corruption—the second "C" in the GOP campaign formula—was also used by candidates at every level. "No Minks,
No Pinks," read placards in evidence at Republican rallies.
Eisenhower did not emphasize the corruption issue in his presidential campaign but the issue generally reinforced his image
of personal integrity. At one point in the campaign, allegations
of a "slush fund" held by GOP vice presidential candidate
Nixon threatened to undo this advantage. But Nixon defended

himself successfully in a masterful (if mawkish) televised speech in which he claimed that his daughters' cocker spaniel "Checkers" was the only possibly illegal gift he had received. The "Checkers speech" not only saved Nixon from being dumped from the Republican ticket but probably further boosted GOP stock in the election.

Though the pollsters hedged their predictions, Eisenhower's rout of Adlai Stevenson on November 4 surprised no one. Besting his opponent by 6.6 million votes, the general carried all but nine states, winning in the electoral college by 442–89. Without another segregationist bolt, as in 1948, the Democrats held the Deep South, but Florida, Tennessee, Texas, and Virginia all went Republican for the first time since 1928. Post-election analyses showed that civil rights played little part in the outcome below the Mason-Dixon Line; more important—even more for the future than for 1952—was the emergence of a new, economically based conservatism friendly to the GOP, especially in the growing cities and suburbs in the Rim South. The GOP tidal wave restored the party to control of both houses of Congress: 48–47 in the Senate (with former Republican Wayne Morse now a declared Independent) and 221–214 in the House.

"K_1C_2" represented a negative mandate—what voters did *not* want. Polls indicated that Korea was the most important issue to voters, but aside from a dramatic pledge by Eisenhower that he would "go to Korea," the campaign provided no illumination of how the GOP would deal with the war. On the communism issue, too, the results were inconclusive. Successful GOP candidates—including Eisenhower—had used the issue, but McCarthy himself, running for reelection to the Senate, ran behind the general in Wisconsin, and three of the most zealously anti-Communist Republican senators up for reelection in 1952 lost. More than anything, as pollster Louis Harris has written, the 1952 election seemed to serve "as a safety valve for [voters'] emotions over the state of the world."

Economic issues were probably as important to the 1952 outcome as any other concern. High taxes and rising prices—

although inflation was never rampant during the Korean War—clearly fueled voter antagonism toward the Democrats. Samuel Lubell, in his now-classic 1952 study, *The Future of American Politics,* emphasized the anger American voters felt over taxes and prices. "Inflation," he wrote presciently on the eve of Eisenhower's election, "has clearly become the breaking point of the Roosevelt coalition." Eisenhower played to such attitudes, taking a conservative line on economic issues throughout his campaign. Explicit in his appeal to the voters was a promise to end inflation and cut taxes, both by ending the war and by cutting "big government" down to size. During the campaign, he spoke with vehemence about "high-handed interference and regulation" and "the alien philosophy that our national destiny lies in the supremacy of government over all." That Truman had managed to keep the national budget balanced seemed not to matter to the voters.

Of great influence on American politics in 1952 was the new phenomenon of television. In 1948, 172,000 American households had TVs; by 1950, the number was 5 million, and by 1952, 15.3 million (this number would more than double by 1956). The televised crime hearings perhaps knocked Truman out of the presidential race in 1952, and helped Joe McCarthy become an overnight political sensation. The new medium also probably helped Eisenhower win the nomination. At the GOP convention, writes Robert E. Gilbert in *Television and Presidential Politics,* ". . . clever maneuvering by the General's lieutenants enabled them to win the sympathy and valuable support of the home audience. This public support . . . proved to be a vital asset to the Eisenhower candidacy." The GOP candidate then used the new concept of spot television commercials to excellent effect in the campaign itself, scheduling them in the middle of such highly popular programs as "I Love Lucy." The president of Batten, Barton, Durstine and Olson, the premier advertising company which handled Eisenhower's media campaign, stated candidly that the idea was to merchandise the candidate's "frankness, honesty and integrity."

On November 18, 1952, the outgoing president and the president-elect met at the White House. Also present were Truman's secretaries of state, defense, and treasury and key foreign policy adviser Averell Harriman. The idea—a novel one in American history—was that the meeting would begin an orderly transition. Unfortunately, so frosty were relations between the two principals that, in the words of Stephen Ambrose (*Eisenhower the President*), "[t]he meeting was stiff, formal, embarrassing, and unrewarding." They did not meet again until Inauguration Day—and then in a very strained atmosphere. Still, the transition, effected by secondary figures on both sides, was smoother than most prior changings of the partisan guard.

The new president was well qualified and knew it. Perhaps because of his greater self-confidence, he seemed to regard Congress more as a coordinate branch of government than as an adversary to be outmaneuvered. Finally, of course, he brought to the White House a view very different from Truman's of the role of government. "Eisenhower brought to the Presidency," Herbert Parmet notes in *Eisenhower and the American Crusades,* "the conviction that the country had had its full measure of new programs during the past twenty years." The nation, it seemed, was shifting gears.

CHAPTER THREE

The Eisenhower Equilibrium, 1953–1956

Unlike his predecessor, Dwight Eisenhower could look forward to working with a basically sympathetic Congress. The 1952 elections had enlarged the conservative coalition by some forty new Republicans in the House and nine in the Senate; these newcomers seemed likely to appreciate their debt to Eisenhower for their election. If the new president was more internationalist in his views than a large portion of congressional Republicans, he could count on support in the area of foreign policy from Democrats. It seemed likely, also, that his prestige would intimidate and convert to his cause all but the most resistant GOP nationalists. The outlook for Ike's success with the Eighty-third Congress was, in other words, quite good—despite the looming threat posed by Joseph McCarthy.

Eisenhower's use of the phrase "middle way" in his first State of the Union message to describe his approach to domestic issues captured the imagination of the public—or at least of the press. Together with his heroic image as a man "above party," the "middle way" imagery led many contemporaries to see "Eisenhower Republicanism" as a departure from traditional GOP policies and as willing acquiescence to the New Deal. Though many historians portray Eisenhower and his policies in this way, there is ample evidence to the contrary.

The Reaffirmation of Republicanism

Eisenhower's record during his first two years in office in working with the GOP-controlled Eighty-third Congress was not one of unrelieved conservatism, but it certainly represented a reaffirmation of traditional Republican values and policies. On one domestic issue after another—economic controls, taxes, power and resources, health policy, agriculture, labor-management relations—Eisenhower staked out traditional GOP positions that broke sharply from the Fair Deal and satisfied his conservative party colleagues. Taft, who took on the duties of Senate majority leader in the few months of life he had remaining in 1953, bridled at Ike's refusal to support tax reductions before federal spending was reduced, but he believed the president sufficiently orthodox so that he went along with White House tax policies. While some of the hidebound GOP tax cutters held out till the end, Eisenhower had his way on the particulars of the tax reduction bill that ultimately passed in August 1954. On the issue of economic controls, too, the president and party conservatives agreed; Korean War controls were dropped in early spring 1953, despite polls that showed the public in favor of retaining them.

Administration farm policy, crafted by the ardently conservative new secretary of agriculture, Ezra Taft Benson, and enacted into law in 1954, contrasted starkly with the programs of high, rigid price supports favored by Fair Deal Democrats. And in power and resource development, Eisenhower's "partnership" policy proved to be nothing more than the conventional GOP preference for private enterprise as opposed to federal action. Eisenhower successfully backed legislation authorizing U.S. participation with Canada in construction of the St. Lawrence Seaway, but on grounds of national security. Other White House actions in 1953–1954 revealed the president's strong aversion to federal activism in resource development. His budget requests for the existing major power installations were dramatically lower than Truman's, and while he did not attempt to dismantle the Tennessee Valley Authority (which he had described as "creeping socialism"), he successfully blocked plans for other federal power development, such as at Hell's Canyon on the Snake River.

In a few areas, Eisenhower seemed somewhat more willing to accommodate to post–New Deal realities than many congressional Republicans. On one such issue—extension of the Social Security system to cover 10.5 million new workers—Eisenhower carried huge GOP majorities in both houses, easily gaining passage for his plan. In other instances where he took less conservative positions, he exhibited a halfheartedness that led to predictable results. "Middle way" administration proposals for health reinsurance (that is, federal underwriting of private health insurance plans), moderate expansion of public housing in cooperation with the private sector, and reform of the Taft-Hartley Act either were dropped in the face of congressional opposition or produced only innocuous legislative results.

Thus, despite all the clamor about "two Republican parties," the president smoothly established himself as his party's leader on the entire gamut of domestic issues. He did this by proving himself a legitimate Republican in his policy preferences, but also by dealing deftly with GOP congressional leaders. Eisenhower's self-proclaimed deference to Congress was a welcome change to Republican senators and congressmen (and even many Democrats) who had been long frustrated by Roosevelt's and Truman's arrogation of power to the White House.

Of great importance was the way the new president immediately developed a productive working relationship with Senator Taft. Though Taft was to serve as majority leader only till mid-June 1953 (and live less than two months beyond that), he exerted an enormously positive influence on fellow GOP legislators to back the president—for instance, on tax policy and on certain key foreign policy questions that emerged early in 1953. Eisenhower appreciated the Ohioan's loyalty and assistance, but he never doubted that he, rather than Taft, ought to lead the party and the nation. Taft, he confided in a memorandum for the files in June 1953, "is so impulsive, and at times so irascible that he can scarcely be classed as a skillful statesman."

Taft's hand-picked successor as majority leader, California's William Knowland, was less helpful. Knowland was a member of the "Asia first" bloc that had bedeviled Truman, an ally (if not a fan) of Joseph McCarthy, an independent and unpredictable voice on domestic issues, and—in James Patterson's phrase—"an aggressive, somewhat humorless man." After Knowland took over as majority leader, Eisenhower frequently blustered in private about the Californian's unconstructive, intractable behavior. But Knowland was basically ineffectual when he opposed the White House; after Taft's death, the GOP conservatives in Congress lacked a strong leader.

In the area of civil rights, it was soon clear that Eisenhower did not intend to take a leadership role. The new president quickly announced he would seek to end segregation in the District of Columbia, to complete the desegregation of the armed forces, and to continue to seek fair employment for blacks, but he was unwilling to press the cause further. Writes Robert Burk, in *The Eisenhower Administration and Black Civil Rights:* "Acutely aware of the political risks inherent in a public leadership role in civil rights, [Eisenhower] preferred to limit his involvement in racial questions to the occasional assertion of general basic principles." Rejecting the idea of another FEPC, for example, the president established a toothless interagency committee on government contracts in August 1953. And although most public facilities in D.C. were nominally desegregated by the end of 1953, the Supreme Court—in the *Thompson* case—was at least as responsible for that as the administration.

The greatest civil rights challenge in the early Eisenhower years was desegregating the nation's public schools. In August 1953, Attorney General Herbert Brownell reported to the president that the Supreme Court had asked the Justice Department to file a brief, as the Truman administration had done, on behalf of the plaintiffs in a set of cases challenging segregation in the public schools that was scheduled soon to come before the Court. Significantly, although the group of cases took its name from a Kansas suit (*Brown v. Board of Education of Topeka*), a District of Columbia case was linked with it, along with five others. Eisenhower, fearful that a ruling against segregation might produce social rupture, wanted to duck the Court request. In December 1953, however, the Justice Department filed a brief essentially opposed to segregation.

As Burk has written, "the greatest contribution of the Eisenhower administration to the Supreme Court's eventual determination [in *Brown*] proved not its 'supplemental brief' but the appointment of Earl Warren as chief justice." It was Warren, named by Eisenhower to succeed the late Chief Justice Fred Vinson in September 1953, who wrote the guiding opinion in *Brown* and succeeded in getting unanimous concurrence in it from his Court colleagues. Eisenhower remarked later that appointing Warren was "the worst damned mistake" he ever made, but in 1953 the selection seemed to be a fair political payoff to the powerful and popular California governor for his help in 1952, and to reflect the president's genuine respect for Warren's abilities. The president wrote to Milton Eisenhower, his brother, a month after he selected Warren that the new chief justice "represents the kind of political, economic and social thinking that I believe we need on the Supreme Court." When Warren spoke for the high court in the *Brown* case on May 17, 1954, declaring "separate but equal" schools unconstitutional, Eisenhower began to doubt his earlier judgment, but it was not until after the Court's very liberal rulings in the mid-1960s that Ike truly began to rue his appointment.

As Eisenhower had feared, the *Brown* case set off a political storm, despite the fact that the Court announced it would entertain further arguments before ruling on implementation (the second ruling came a year later). Southern conservatives were outraged, including some of Eisenhower's friends, such as Governors James Byrnes of South Carolina and Alan Shivers of Texas. Many held the president personally responsible, since he had appointed Warren. Subversion was also suspected; the justices, charged Mississippi's segregationist Senator James Eastland, had been "indoctrinated and brainwashed by the Left-wing pressure groups." This reaction foreshadowed the later tendency of conservatives to equate support for desegregation with Communism.

Eisenhower's lack of enthusiasm for the *Brown* decision was obvious. In his first press conference after the ruling, he pledged to "uphold the Constitutional process," but slipped in some words of praise for Governor Byrnes's moderate statement opposing the decision. The administration refrained from investigating any segregation complaints while awaiting the Court's implementation decision. Meanwhile, desegregation efforts across the nation proceeded haltingly at best. Among the seventeen states where schools were legally segregated in 1954, only a few border states made prompt starts; in the District of Columbia, 64 percent of all public schools continued to be at least 98 percent one race or the other in 1954–1955, with another 18 percent consisting of at least nine-tenths one race. Disturbances accompanying early desegregation efforts in the politically moderate border states presaged much greater trouble in Dixie after the anticipated implementation ruling. But, given the magnitude of the other dramas unfolding in Washington in 1954, the school desegregation issue—almost incredibly, in retrospect—could not long command the front pages of the nation's newspapers, or even the attention of its politicians.

A New Foreign Policy?

Eisenhower had run for the presidency in 1952 because of his deep convictions about American foreign policy. At least some conflict between the White House and Capitol Hill seemed inevitable, as conservative Republicans hoped for (and expected) a radical departure from the policies of Truman and Acheson. Yet Eisenhower chose not to preside over a "new" foreign policy. He bested the GOP Right on virtually every foreign policy issue that divided them during 1953–1954. By the time the Eighty-third Congress adjourned, the nationalist bloc had shrunk from over 50 percent of the Republican membership to about 25 percent in each house.

The issue demanding immediate attention in early 1953 was the Korean War. A few weeks after his election, Eisenhower fulfilled his campaign promise to visit the battlefront in Korea. He returned utterly convinced that the war must end, and quickly. Since his military experience led him to reject either a large-scale frontal assault or a continuing series of small battles, he believed serious negotiations to be the only acceptable option. To move the nearly two-year-old peace talks along and to preempt opposition from the Republican right, Eisenhower introduced the threat of escalation if the enemy continued to be uncooperative. "We face an enemy whom we cannot hope to impress by words, however eloquent," he remarked following the Korea trip, "but only by deeds—executed under circumstances of our own choosing." The reference was clear: atomic weapons might be used.

Armistice talks resumed in earnest in April 1953, accompanied by an exchange of wounded prisoners by the two sides. Secretary of State John Foster Dulles was unenthusiastic about continuing the armistice talks, believing the United States could do better than a cease fire at the thirty-eighth parallel, but Eisenhower was adamant that it would be "impossible to call off the armistice and go to war again in Korea." While reining in South Korean leader Syngman Rhee, who favored an all-out attack on North Korea, the president relied on the Chinese Communists' fears of American atomic weapons to move the talks toward successful conclusion. Finally, on June 4, the Chinese presented a truce proposal that included a prisoner-exchange provision likely to satisfy the United Nations.

When Rhee tried to sabotage the armistice plan by unilaterally releasing 25,000 North Korean and Chinese prisoners held by the South, thus undermining possibilities for orderly repatriation, he had many champions among congressional Republicans. But statements of support for Rhee by such "Asia-firsters" as Senators Bridges, Knowland, and H. Alexander Smith (New Jersey) failed to dissuade the administration. Through General Mark Clark, Eisenhower made clear to Rhee that he had no choice but to agree to the plan; postwar reconstruction funds and a mutual security agreement with the United States were held out to South Korea as future rewards if it cooperated. On July 26, 1953, the Korean agreement was signed, and the guns at last fell silent. "The armistice was, despite its reception," writes Ambrose, "one of Eisenhower's greatest achievements. . . . [D]espite great opposition from his own party, from his Secretary of State, and from Syngman Rhee, he had ended the war six months after taking office."

Congressional Democrats had remained largely passive observers as Eisenhower ended the fighting in Korea. Occasionally, however, they spoke out. Lyndon Johnson and Richard Russell, invited to accompany administration leaders on a trip to Korea after the armistice, declined on grounds that Congress was still in session. And in late December, a number of Senate Democrats publicly questioned the wisdom of Eisenhower's decision to reduce the American forces in Korea. The withdrawal was "a little premature," remarked Fulbright; it "smacks of appeasement," said Russell.

The general issue of defense needs versus budget constraints caused Eisenhower serious problems with the Democrats. Controversy centered on the defense policy unveiled by Eisenhower. This "New Look" policy was intended to cut costs even while beefing up American military capabilities. In spring 1953, Eisenhower sent Congress a defense budget $5.1 billion less than Truman's final proposed budget. Since all the initial cuts were to be in the air force budget, Democratic airpower advocates, led by freshman Senator (and former secretary of the air force) Stuart Symington of Missouri, immediately voiced loud opposition. Echoing earlier Republican denunciations of Acheson, Democratic Congressman Melvin Price of Illinois described the reduced budget as an "invitation" to enemy attack.

The true shape of the New Look became clearer in late 1953. "Effectiveness with economy" was to be achieved through cuts in conventional forces rather than reductions in airpower; in fact, within a smaller overall defense budget, air defense was to receive by far the greatest emphasis. This represented a significant shift from Truman's defense policy, and a sharp reduction in conventional military capability. Criticisms were widely varied; air enthusiasts complained about the absolute reductions in air force spending, while a number of other powerful Democrats leveled attacks at the administration's over-reliance on air-atomic power and penny-pinching approach to defense in general.

Despite its drawbacks, the New Look was at least consistent with the sometimes contradictory GOP propensities for a strong unilateral defense arm and a reduced budget. Congressional Republicans, therefore, largely supported the president's new approach. The public, too, was in Eisenhower's corner. In late July 1953, the Gallup poll reported that a majority of all Americans questioned (including 69 percent of the Republicans, and 44 percent of the Democrats) believed that the New Look did not present a threat to American national security—that "only waste and extravagance have been cut out of the budget."

Democratic attacks on Eisenhower's defense policies intensified in January 1954, following Secretary of State Dulles's public pronouncement of the doctrine of "massive retaliation." The New Look emphasis on airpower, Dulles explained, gave the United States the capacity for instant, massive retaliation against an enemy—"maximum deterrent at bearable cost." Leading Democrats expressed strong opposition to the secretary's unsubtle implication that atomic weapons might be used in a pinch. Writing to Adlai Stevenson, Averell Harriman deplored the administration's "psychopathic urge to have a new policy." The public, however, remained on the administration's side: when queried in September 1954, 64 percent of those questioned believed that the country was in a better position than it had been two years earlier to defend itself.

During Eisenhower's second year in the White House, the Democrats became increasingly critical of the administration on specific foreign policy issues—particularly its handling of the Indochina crisis. In April, the French, long recipients of American aid for their efforts to retain control of their colonies in Indochina, faced imminent defeat at the hands of the nationalist pro-Communist Viet Minh forces there. Their armies trapped in a mountainous redoubt at Dien Bien Phu, the French appealed to Eisenhower for military assistance—nuclear, if possible. Such a reaction was briefly considered in a meeting with congressional leaders called by Dulles. At the meeting Lyndon Johnson and another Democratic senator, Earl Clements of Kentucky, asked questions sufficiently probing to make the administration doubly cautious about either intervening directly or seeking a congressional resolution authorizing intervention.

By summer, the military crisis was resolved, with the United States standing aside while the French negotiated terms for their ignominious withdrawal from Indochina. The resulting Geneva Accords barred the introduction of any further troops or military advisers by outside powers, but not before Eisenhower had dispatched an additional 200 American "technicians" to assist the pro-French Vietnamese forces in the southern half who were doing battle against the Viet Minh. Leading Democrats, including many southerners, objected to this administration action as unnecessary and provocative. "We are going to war," Senator John Stennis of Mississippi warned, "inch by inch." Other Democrats, such as young John F. Kennedy of Massachusetts and Hubert Humphrey, objected that the United States was ignoring the all-important question of colonialism in the Southeast Asian conflict. The issue, said Humphrey, should not be made "one of white man versus Asiatic."

That clear-cut contest did not emerge in the 1950s, of course—the Vietnam War would result from larger commitments by Democratic presidents in the 1960s. But the growing tendency of Eisenhower-Dulles policies to enmesh the United States in the politics of the Far East, symbolized by the Southeast Asian Treaty Organization (SEATO), to which the administration pledged the nation in September 1954, coupled with the implied threat of atomic diplomacy in the "massive retaliation" doctrine, fueled Democratic criticisms. Meanwhile, the administration drew fire from the "Asia first" bloc in the GOP as well, for different reasons. According to Knowland and other Old Guard Republicans, the Geneva Accords (supported, but not formally signed, by the United States) were appeasement. Not satisfied that Eisenhower and Dulles were doing much more than Truman and Acheson had, they wanted stronger action in China.

The "Asia first" bloc nearly got its wish in the fall of 1954, as crisis erupted in September over the Communist Chinese shelling of the offshore islands of Quemoy and Matsu. Garrisoned by Nationalist forces loyal to Chiang Kai-shek, these small islands had always been part of China, unlike Formosa. They thus had symbolic importance to both Chinese regimes. In mid-September, the president met with Dulles and the Joint Chiefs of Staff (JCS) in Denver, where he was vacationing, to chart a course for American action. "[I]f we attack China," Eisenhower told the assembled brainpower, "we're not going to impose limits on our military actions, as in Korea." The crisis dragged on through the fall, with several Democrats increasing their public criticisms of "massive retaliation" as both a danger to, yet in some ways an inhibition of American capability to respond to crises such as the Quemoy-Matsu shelling. Eisenhower held firm against the hawkish pressures of Dulles and JCS Chief Arthur Radford, deciding against a military response. But the chances for future American involvement in Asia seemed to increase when in December 1954 the administration signed a mutual defense treaty with Chiang's Nationalist government.

Eisenhower threaded his way carefully through a succession of potentially explosive international crises in 1953–1954, countering the vociferous criticisms of Democrats and GOP nationalists through a combination of restraint, good judgment, and a tendency to shield American actions abroad from congressional scrutiny by using the CIA in new, more aggressive ways. This last tactic was employed to deal with perceived Communist threats in Iran in 1953 and Guatemala in 1954. That both CIA ventures succeeded—restoring the shah to power in Iran, and ousting the left-leaning Jacobo Arbenz Guzman in Guatemala—undoubtedly confirmed Eisenhower's sense that he could accomplish much of what he wanted to do in the world without congressional sniping by coupling restraint in his public pronouncements with purposeful covert actions.

There was, however, one threat to Eisenhower's exercise of power in foreign affairs that he felt he had to lay to rest at the beginning of his presidency. The Bricker Amendment, introduced by Old Guard Republican John Bricker in 1951, aimed to curtail the president's power to make treaties and enter into executive agreements. Congressional control over such agreements was to be ensured, under Bricker's proposal, by the "which clause," stipulating that "a treaty shall become effective as internal law in the United States only through legislation which would be valid in the absence of a treaty." Since the definition of "internal law" remained unclear, the clause gave Congress a virtually unlimited power to second-guess not only executive agreements, but also duly ratified treaties.

In introducing his measure in 1951, Bricker had not disguised his partisan motives, noting in a magazine article that the amendment would help to keep the Truman administration from agreeing to certain proposed international covenants of "distinctly scarlet hue." On the Senate floor, he took a loftier approach. "The constitutional power of Congress to determine American foreign policy is at stake," he told the Senate. "It is our duty to preserve that power against presidential encroachment." In January 1953, as the new Republican Congress convened and the inauguration of a GOP president was imminent,

Bricker reintroduced his amendment. The measure, Senate Joint Resolution 1, had sixty-four cosponsors, just enough to produce the required two-thirds vote for passage in the upper house. Among the cosponsors were forty-five Republicans and nineteen Democrats. Bricker and his Republican colleagues felt justified in pressing the amendment on the new administration since the 1952 GOP platform had included a plank advocating it. They were motivated also by lurking suspicions that Eisenhower might prove little different from Truman in his basic foreign policy instincts.

Eisenhower wavered briefly, but he soon resolved to oppose what he came to regard as a "silly" measure. Herbert Brownell later explained that the president's change of heart occurred "as his own experience, dealing with foreign nations as President developed. . . ." Once having arrived at his position, Eisenhower took a very active role, together with Dulles and Brownell, in trying to negotiate with Bricker. By mid-1953, however, he grew weary of the silver-haired Ohio senator who, he believed, viewed the amendment "as his one hope of achieving at least a faint immortality in American history." The seemingly endless negotiating sessions produced no common ground on the measure. In early February 1954, with the amendment fight nearing conclusion in the Senate, Eisenhower remarked in exasperation that "if it's true that when you die the things that bothered you most are engraved on your skull, I'm sure I'll have there the mud and dirt of France during invasion and the name of Senator Bricker."

Ultimately, Eisenhower orchestrated a successful strategy for derailing the amendment. Rejecting Dulles's suggestion of fighting the measure on the grounds that it would subordinate the executive branch to Congress, the president urged a fight based on the need for the chief executive to have maneuvering room in waging the Cold War. This tactic skirted the sensitive issue of the balance of power between the two branches, and tapped into the strong anti-Communist feelings of most supporters of Bricker's proposal. In order to prevail, the administration had to convert some of the cosponsors to its side.

With assistance from Senator Alexander Wiley of Wisconsin, who chaired the Foreign Relations Committee, White House personnel lobbied potential Republican waverers. The administration also showed sensitivity to the feelings of key Democrats. "Senator George [Democrat of Georgia] probably will help," the president's press secretary accurately predicted in his diary in late January. "[The] Democrats will want some credit for 'saving the Constitution' and we'll give them that."

In the end, it was Senator George who offered the substitute amendment for Bricker's on which the decisive roll-call vote was taken. The result was a division of 60–31 for the George substitute—one vote short of passage. On the crucial roll call, eleven Republican cosponsors (and one Democrat) shifted to vote for the administration position. Though Bricker later tried to revive his amendment, the February 1954 roll calls were the last ever taken on the measure. Eisenhower had won a conclusive victory in the battle to control the nation's foreign policy.

The End of McCarthyism

Of all the problems Eisenhower faced in his first two years in the White House, none was as troubling as McCarthyism. Although the new president was not sympathetic to the Wisconsin senator's actions, the 1952 Republican platform had contained stridently anti-Communist language. The party victory seemed to promise a heyday for red hunters. In January 1953, as David Oshinsky has written, "a mad scramble ensued [in Congress] over control and direction of the Communist issue." When McCarthy emerged from the fray with the chairmanship of the Government Operations Committee, including its $200,000 annual budget and the right to chair the Subcommittee on Investigations, it was clear he had won the struggle. "No one can push me out of anything," he remarked in reply to reports that the GOP leadership wanted to shift power to investigate subversion to some other, more docile, senator. "I am not retiring from the field of exposing Communists."

The administration triumphed in its first two skirmishes with McCarthy. In early March 1953, the White House managed at the last minute to avert a showdown with McCarthy, Bricker, Jenner, and other Old Guard Republicans over a proposed resolution repudiating the Yalta agreements, which they viewed as an immoral "give-away" of Eastern Europe to the Soviets. Eisenhower and Dulles believed that such a resolution would imperil certain of the desirable outcomes of Yalta, such as American occupation rights in Berlin, and would unnecessarily alienate the Democrats. Upon the death of Soviet leader Josef Stalin, the administration persuaded GOP congressional leaders to shelve the proposal in order not to disturb United States-Soviet relations at such a critical moment. Another presidential victory occurred just a few weeks later when, with help from Senator Taft, the president secured a lopsidedly positive vote confirming his nomination of Charles E. Bohlen to be ambassador to Russia. Bohlen's earlier service in Roosevelt's delegation to Yalta made him anathema to McCarthy and his supporters. Taft's intercession at a critical moment, including his testimony to the Senate after reading FBI files on Bohlen, saved the day for the White House, and Bohlen was confirmed 74–13. Eleven Republicans voted nay, including McCarthy, Bricker, Hickenlooper, and Everett Dirksen.

These two White House victories, however, failed to halt McCarthy's investigative crusade against "subversives" in governmental agencies. A Senate subcommittee probe of his conduct in 1952 had come to nothing. Thus cleared, in February 1953 McCarthy announced plans to investigate the Voice of America. From those hearings, which extended through March, the senator moved on to an inquiry into the International Information Agency, finishing up in July. The result, according to Oshinsky, was that the IIA was left "in ruins" and morale in the State Department at a low ebb.

Dulles, running scared before McCarthy, worsened the situation by giving a virtual free hand to Scott McLeod, a McCarthy protégé who served as chief security officer for the State Department. In April, McLeod's red hunt was given a distinct assist by Eisenhower, who issued Executive Order 10450, which broadened the grounds for dismissal of federal employees. It was no longer necessary to prove disloyalty; those who posed "security risks" were now subject to firing. The expanded category could include alcoholics, homosexuals, and those merely inclined to talk too much. This order stimulated sharp criticisms about the president's lack of backbone in dealing with McCarthy.

The anti-Communist crusade was big news in 1953. The general tone was set by President Eisenhower's firm refusal to grant a pardon to Julius and Ethel Rosenberg; convicted of atomic espionage in a highly dramatic case two years earlier, they were executed in June. Meanwhile, responsible Republican congressional leaders were compliant in the face of McCarthy's unethical and unrestrained behavior. "Only Taft and Nixon seemed able to reach him," writes Oshinsky, "and Taft was now too sick to try." In September, the Wisconsin senator launched what would turn out to be a protracted final act in his demagogic crusade: an inquiry into charges of subversive activities at Fort Monmouth, New Jersey. After several weeks of relatively uneventful committee sessions on Fort Monmouth, McCarthy opened up public hearings in late November.

At this point, the administration was coming under fire from McCarthy's critics, not only for failing to bridle the senator, but also for its own zealous approach to ferreting out the "disloyal." In early November, Brownell publicly charged that Truman had given a sensitive diplomatic appointment to a man (Harry Dexter White) about whose loyalty the FBI had raised questions. Truman angrily responded in a televised speech, explaining that the appointment had already been made before the FBI submitted its report and that the FBI had agreed that he should not revoke White's appointment. The former president went on, scowling, to charge that "the present Administration has fully embraced, for political advantage, McCarthyism."

Stung by the former president's accusation and unhappy

with McCarthy for taking on so cherished an institution as the U.S. Army, Eisenhower moved towards actively opposing McCarthy. His increasingly sharp comments within White House circles were accompanied by a strong public statement, in his press conference of December 3, 1953, that "fear of Communists actively undermining our government" would *not* be a campaign issue in 1954. Administration heavyweights, including Vice President Nixon and Attorney General Brownell, were detailed to put pressure on McCarthy to end or at least deescalate his Fort Monmouth investigation. At first the White House used a combination of flattery and assurances of its own strong anti-Communist credentials. By January 1954, however, the strategy shifted, as the administration worked with army counsel John Adams to bring countercharges against McCarthy for attempting to exert improper influence on behalf of a wealthy young draftee, David Schine, a close friend of the senator's chief counsel, Roy Cohn.

Denouement was near. At this point, McCarthy changed his tactics, focusing his army probe on a single case: the promotion of Captain Irving Peress by authorities at Fort Kilmer, despite Peress's earlier refusal to comment regarding his previous participation in subversive organizations. From the Peress case ("who promoted Peress?" he droned endlessly through the hearings in January and February 1954), McCarthy argued that the army lacked a policy for dealing with security risks. On February 18, he overstepped the bounds of what Eisenhower was willing to tolerate, accusing Peress's former commanding officer, the much-decorated General Ralph Zwicker, of being "not fit to wear [the army] uniform." When Secretary of the Army Robert Stevens interceded to protect Zwicker and became a target himself for McCarthy's abuse, the administration became fully engaged. First, Nixon set up a luncheon between the antagonists, McCarthy and Stevens, attended also by Senators Dirksen and Karl Mundt, to try to work out a settlement, but with no success. Then, on March 3, Eisenhower came to the defense of Zwicker, calling on congressional Republicans to make sure the army hearings were conducted fairly.

In retrospect, it is clear that McCarthy's collapse began in early March 1954. At that point, according to Oshinsky, "the first signs of Republican resistance [to McCarthy] had begun to appear," as the Wisconsin legislator's irresponsible and ruthless tactics finally began to seem too much. It was also then that the medium of television weighed in against the senator, in the form of Edward R. Murrow's popular program, *See It Now*. "This is not time for men who oppose Senator McCarthy's methods to keep quiet," Murrow admonished his viewers in his impassioned closing to a show he had devoted entirely to McCarthy's exploits. "The actions of the junior senator from Wisconsin have caused alarm and dismay amongst our allies abroad and given considerable comfort to our enemies, and whose fault is that . . . ? Cassius was right: 'The fault, dear Brutus, is not in our stars but in ourselves.'" CBS switchboards in Los Angeles, Washington, Milwaukee, Chicago, and other cities lit up immediately after the show. Affiliates in all major cities reported sentiment to be over-whelmingly in support of Murrow's pillorying of McCarthy and his methods.

Less noticed at the time, but perhaps more ominous, was a speech delivered in the Senate on the same day as Murrow's broadcast by the usually mild-mannered Ralph Flanders, a Vermont Republican. Flanders treated McCarthy derisively rather than with venom, characterizing the furor over Peress in mocking terms: "He [McCarthy] dons his war paint. He goes into his war dance. He emits war whoops. He goes forth to battle and proudly returns with the scalp of a pink dentist." The combination of Murrow's solemn denunciations and Flanders's mockery was potentially devastating.

From this point forward, McCarthy did more damage to himself than did any of his growing band of foes. On April 6, Murrow gave him air time to answer the earlier broadcast. "It was as though the senator's worst enemy had done him in," wrote CBS executive Fred Friendly later, "—which indeed was the case. It was twenty-five minutes of unrelieved McCarthy." Afterwards, according to Friendly, CBS's "mail continued to run in Murrow's favor ..., but the ratio did drop down to only two to one." In the televised army hearings, which ran from late April through mid-June, the senator eventually fared even worse. When the hearings ended after seventy-two sessions, the specific issues had not been resolved. But McCarthy's future had. The Gallup poll recorded steady erosion in his base of support, as his public approval rating declined from 50 percent in January 1954, to 46 percent in March, down to 38 percent in April, and then to 34 percent in June. From April on, a plurality of those questioned gave him a frankly unfavorable rating.

By June 9, when the gritty special counsel to the army, Boston lawyer Joseph Welch, quietly leveled his memorable accusation at McCarthy ("Have you no sense of decency, sir, at long last?"), the game was lost for McCarthy. Along the way, Eisenhower had stiffened his position considerably, most notably in a May 17 directive to Secretary of Defense Charles Wilson not to release to McCarthy any materials related to counsel given to the president by his advisers. His sweeping claim of "executive privilege," though unprecedented in its scope, drew little objection. "[F]ew noticed, and fewer commented on Eisenhower's boldness in establishing" the concept, writes Ambrose, "which quickly came to be regarded as traditional."

The final act of the McCarthy drama began with another Senate speech by Senator Flanders on June 2, this one sharper than his speech three months earlier. McCarthy, according to Flanders, was the cause of divisiveness throughout national life. "Were the junior Senator from Wisconsin in the pay of Communists," he declared, "he could not have done a better job for them." In late July, with McCarthy still salving his wounds from the recently ended televised hearings, Flanders introduced S. 231, a bill to strip McCarthy of his committee chairmanships. Because such an action threatened the hallowed Senate principle of seniority, influential Republicans and southern Democrats urged Flanders to substitute a simple resolution calling for censure, which he did. On August 7, 1954, the motion to censure was referred to a special six-man committee, by a vote of 75–12. Interestingly, the strongest critics of McCarthy—such as Flanders and Fulbright—voted no on this compromise proposal, believing it too weak.

Chaired by the eminently respectable Arthur Watkins of Utah, the committee included two southerners (Mississippi's John Stennis and Sam Ervin of North Carolina), a conservative western Democrat (Edwin Johnston of Colorado), and two orthodox farm-belt Republicans not especially close to McCarthy (Frank Carlson of Kansas and Francis Case of South Dakota). The committee's report was not due until after the November congressional elections.

McCarthy was on his way down, but one more monument to anticommunism remained to be erected by the Eighty-third Congress: the Communist Control Act of 1954. This law yoked together a proposal by McCarthyite GOP Senator John Marshall Butler of Maryland (who had vanquished Tydings in 1950) with a harsh measure offered by liberal Democrats as a substitute. Butler's original bill barred any member of a Communist organization from holding office in a labor organization and denied access to the National Labor Relations Board to "Communist-infiltrated" organizations. The liberals' contribution to the law, written by Hubert Humphrey, declared the Communist party not to be a party, but the "agency of a hostile power," and made its adherents subject to penalties outlined in the McCarran Internal Security Act of 1950. For the record, the administration opposed the bill. Attorney General Brownell contended that the various sections would nullify the McCarran Act's requirement that members of the Communist party register as such, and questioned the proposal's overall constitutionality. No matter; with near unanimity (79–0 in the Senate, and 265–2 in the House), Congress adopted the monstrosity and Eisenhower signed it. "The legislative history of the Communist Control Act," observes Richard Fried in *Men Against McCarthy,* "attested to one lawmaker's dictum that this was 'not a normal time.' "

The politicians, at least, perceived communism to be an

important issue in the 1954 elections. In June, Democratic National Committee Chairman Stephen Mitchell predicted that the GOP would "use the President to smile and McCarthy to smear" in the fall campaigns. Although the Wisconsin senator was long past his zenith by the time campaigning began in earnest, the prediction was partially on target. Republican candidates focused on the Communist issue, helped along by the Civil Service Commission's fortuitously timed announcement in mid-October that nearly 7,000 "security risks" had been dismissed in the previous year. "How Red is John Carroll?" asked GOP senatorial candidate Gordon Allott about his Democratic opponent for the Colorado seat. In Wyoming, Republican strategists labeled Democratic Senate candidate Joseph O'Mahoney "foreign agent 783," a sinister-sounding reference to O'Mahoney's entirely legitimate registration as legal representative for Cuban sugar interests. Leading the red baiting, Vice President Nixon visited ninety-five cities in thirty states, boasting that Eisenhower had "put the Reds on the run," and asserting that the Communist party "had determined to conduct its program within the Democratic party." "McCarthyism in a white collar," a disgusted Adlai Stevenson remarked of Nixon's methods.

The president himself jumped into the fray on October 8, declaring in a press conference that "a cold war of partisan politics" would result if the Democrats won control of Congress. Ignoring the earlier advice of Henry Cabot Lodge that the "1954 election should *not* be regarded as a national election" or "a vote of confidence," Eisenhower traveled over 10,000 miles, delivering over forty campaign speeches (mostly in the East). He concentrated on administration achievements—ending the Korean War, reducing federal spending, cutting taxes—and stressed the generally prosperous state of the economy. He spoke with particular pride about reducing the scope of government, a line readily embraced by many Republican congressional candidates. Nixon, who also warmed to this theme, claimed the GOP had destroyed the "blueprint for socializing America" which had existed prior to 1952.

The election results, foreseen by the polls and the media, were a blow to the GOP, as the party lost control of Congress. The Democrats gained a net of two Senate seats (giving them control by 48 to 47, with lone Independent Wayne Morse pledged to vote with them) and nineteen House seats, giving them a 232–203 margin in that chamber. Such important liberal Democrats as Paul Douglas, Hubert Humphrey, Estes Kefauver, and James Murray (Montana) were returned to the Senate, and liberals Pat McNamara (Michigan) and Richard Neuberger (Oregon) now joined them. Big Democratic winners in gubernatorial races included Averell Harriman in New York and Orville Freeman in Minnesota, as well as popular incumbent G. Mennen Williams in Michigan. A number of prominent Republicans survived, including Senators Styles Bridges, Karl Mundt, Leverett Saltonstall (Massachusetts), and Margaret Chase Smith.

For all the furor, communism seemed to have played little role in the outcome. "Across the country, the issues were diffuse . . . ," concludes Fried. "Communists-in-government was not a very salient issue to the 1954 electorate." He cites one public opinion study that showed only 3 percent of the sample population voluntarily praising the GOP for "getting Communists out of government." McCarthy himself, on the brink of political extinction and in ill health, did not campaign at all. The real issues operating in 1954 seem to have been chronic unemployment in such key states as Kentucky, Illinois, Michigan, Pennsylvania, and West Virginia, and falling farm prices that damaged the GOP in dairy farming states. Peace, however, and the general perception that Eisenhower's foreign policy was successful, cushioned the GOP from greater losses, averting an embarrassing negative mandate on the two-year-old administration.

After the elections, the lame duck Eighty-third Congress still had to act on the report of the Watkins Committee concerning McCarthy. The forty-thousand-word report recommended censure on two counts: McCarthy's verbal abuse of General Zwicker and his contempt of the Senate committee that had looked into his earlier campaign activities. Senator Dirksen tried to get McCarthy to apologize to at least one colleague he had blatantly insulted, but McCarthy refused, telling Dirksen, "I don't crawl. I learned to fight in an alley. That's all I know."

By this time, it was probably too late to compromise. On December 2, 1954, the Senate voted, 67-22, to "condemn" McCarthy's behavior on two counts. The Zwicker charge was dropped, but substantiated was a count of verbal abuse of Senator Watkins and the special committee. Senate Republicans divided evenly on the roll call (22-22), with McCarthy's supporters in the end being virtually the same Old Guard legislators who had supported the Bricker Amendment earlier in the year. The Democrats, gleeful at the GOP's discomfiture, voted 45-0 to condemn McCarthy. The day after the vote, Eisenhower ostentatiously invited Watkins to the White House to congratulate him for having "handled a tough job like a champion."

McCarthy, McCarthyism, and Eisenhower's handling of both have been subjects of much attention from historians. After early assessments that McCarthyism was a mass movement gone sour, a seeming consensus has evolved, since publication of Michael Paul Rogin's *The Intellectuals and McCarthy* in 1967, that it was—as Robert Griffith has written—a product "of the normal operation of American politics." McCarthy's triumph, concludes Griffith in *The Politics of Fear: Joseph R. McCarthy and the Senate,* "was the consequence of Republican partisanship and, after 1950, of Democratic acquiescence." The more recent works on McCarthyism by Fried, Oshinsky, and Thomas Reeves (*The Life and Times of Joe McCarthy*) do not question such an interpretation, though Oshinsky, especially, emphasizes anew the significance of McCarthy himself: "McCarthy *was* unique. He had competitors but no equals. . . . He knew how to use the media. He crafted a very effective public image. And he was adept at probing the weak spots of opponents."

Just as historians have generally emphasized the systemic,

political reasons for McCarthy's successes, they have attrib-
uted the decline of the "-ism" to broad forces more than to
any immediate cause. Fried, for example, cites "a slackening
of cold-war tensions, a subtle downward shift in his popularity,
a related decline in fear on the part of his colleagues." But
McCarthy's mistake in "crossing" Eisenhower by attacking the
army was clearly crucial as well. Eisenhower's handling of
McCarthyism still invites debate. Political scientist Fred I.
Greenstein, in *The Hidden-Hand Presidency: Eisenhower as
Leader,* argues that the president played a deft and instrumental behind-the-scenes role in undoing McCarthy, but no
other scholar has gone so far. Most still tend to portray Eisenhower as reluctant to take the senator on. His reluctance,
in Griffith's view, "arose in part from his realistic, if cynical,
respect for McCarthy's support among Senate Republicans,
in part from his personal dislike for the philippic mode. It
also derived, however, from his sophisticated analysis of the
relationships between McCarthy, the media, and the presidency." Fried contends that Eisenhower's evocation of "executive privilege" as the vehicle for finally confronting Mc-
Carthy was "less than inspirational."

On balance, the analysis offered by Oshinsky seems both
fair and accurate. Eisenhower, he writes, "was not about to
battle McCarthy in public; that would always be out of the
question." But in early 1954, "he was ready, at long last, to
assume the decision-making responsibilities that had so divided his staff. From this point forward, there would be no
more appeasement of McCarthy. The policy, instead, would
be one of firm but quiet resistance, intended to isolate and
embarrass the senator without resorting to fits of public dis-
pleasure." As was so often true for Eisenhower, his tactics
worked.

"[I]t is thought possible," commented the astute journalist
Richard Rovere in November 1954, "that there will be considerably less of the Hippodrome about the new Congress than
there has been for many years. The expectation in most quar-
ters . . . is for a smoother, quieter time than we have had at

any time since the end of the war." The Korean War was ended, the Bricker Amendment defeated, the New Look policy firmly established, and McCarthy undone. In a strange way, the restoration of narrow Democratic majorities in Congress to counter the Republican president seemed to augur less rather than more conflict. "We're going to cooperate like all getout," a victorious Democrat told *Newsweek* after the 1954 elections. After more than five years of useless partisan combat, true equilibrium seemed at hand.

The Cooptation of Congress

In his third State of the Union message, delivered on January 6, 1955, Eisenhower extended an olive branch to the new Democratic Congress. The fact that the two branches were controlled by opposite parties, he stated, "places both parties on trial before the American people." The president continued, "In less perilous days of the past, division of governmental responsibility among our great parties has produced a paralyzing indecision. We must not let this happen in our time. We must avoid a paralysis of the will for peace and international security."

Eisenhower's strategy for averting paralysis, unveiled within two weeks of these remarks, no doubt surprised many Democrats who had looked forward, naively, to a true partnership. It emerged in the form of the Formosa Resolution, the first of two "area resolutions" which together, in their sweeping delegation of the war-making authority, gave the president unprecedented latitude to ignore those whom he had promised to consult. The Formosa Resolution of 1955 and the Middle East Resolution of 1957, following on Eisenhower's defeat of the Bricker Amendment, left the executive branch in clear control of foreign policy.

Crisis had been brewing in the Formosa Straits since September 1954, when the Communist Chinese had begun shelling the Quemoy island group. Eisenhower gave moral support to Chiang Kai-shek's retaliatory aerial bombardment of the responsible artillery positions, but stood fast against Dulles's urgings that the United States should bomb the mainland. In the late months of 1954, the Formosan situation settled into a war of nerves, with each of the Chinese governments building up its military strength. When Communist shellings intensified again in mid-January 1955, Eisenhower decided to seek broad authorization for action.

On January 20, Secretary of State Dulles was dispatched to Capitol Hill to brief the congressional leadership, without seeking their advice. Four days later, Eisenhower sent a special message to the Congress requesting a first-ever "area resolution"—a measure authorizing the president "to employ the Armed Forces of the United States as he deems necessary" in a specified part of the world. Many observers ascribed Eisenhower's request to his willingness to defer to Congress, asking for authority he did not feel he had, but he was also preempting later congressional criticism and gaining unilateral control over the nature of the American response in Formosa.

In his special message, the president vaguely suggested that he might already possess the powers in question, but promised that any "authority that may be accorded by Congress would be used only in situations which are recognizable as part of, or definite preliminaries to, an attack against the main positions of Formosa and the Pescadores." Those "main positions" received no further clarification. The secretary of state was equally imprecise on the legal issue. Since a divisive battle in Congress would be counterproductive, Dulles asked GOP legislators not to "needle" their Democratic colleagues by contrasting Eisenhower's adherence to "constitutional" process with Truman's actions in the Korean War. Meanwhile, the president played down the significance of the resolution, rejecting a suggestion from Senator Knowland that he appear in person before Congress because, he said, such an action "would indicate a policy, purpose [and] possible action that is greater than we intend." He wanted to keep the request as "routine" as possible.

Congress responded as the president hoped it would. The

Formosa Resolution sailed through the House, 410-3. In the Senate, only a small number of Democrats opposed it. After Herbert Lehman (New York) tried unsuccessfully to confine the authorization of American force to the defense of only Formosa and the Pescadores, the resolution passed in the Senate by a vote of 85-3.

With the Formosa crisis dragging on, the Senate also quickly ratified two other measures relating to China, a mutual assistance treaty with Nationalist China and United States participation in SEATO. The nearly unanimous Democratic support for these two measures reflected effective work by the party's congressional leadership, rather than genuine support. A number of party members began to grumble in private. "It made me most unhappy," wrote Morse disgustedly, "to find out that so many members of the Senate were willing to admit in cloakroom discussions that they would like to have joined in opposing the Resolution and Treaty, but that they simply had to go along with the Democratic leadership."

"The beauty of Eisenhower's policy," writes Robert Divine in *Eisenhower and the Cold War,* "is that to this day no one can be sure whether or not he would have responded militarily to an invasion of the offshore islands, and whether he would have used nuclear weapons." He seemed to threaten the latter, and it was quite possibly that implied threat that brought at least a temporary end to the crisis in late April. The president had come through a winner, having both faced down the Communist aggressors and discovered a device that could (and would) be used in the future to secure a virtual free hand for the presidency in the use of military forces.

While the administration worked to avoid partisan discord over its China policy, congressional Democrats became angry over the almost extraneous issue of publication of the records of the 1945 Yalta conference. Yalta remained for many Old Guard Republicans a symbol of all that had been wrong with Roosevelt's and Truman's handling of foreign policy. By publishing the complete records of the conference, conservatives hoped to reveal naiveté, if not duplicity, on the part of

FDR and the American entourage. Under continuing pressure from the party's congressional wing, the administration agreed to publish the proceedings and make them available for use by the Foreign Relations Committee.

Unfortunately for the cause of interparty harmony, however, the Yalta Papers were "leaked" to the *New York Times*. When angry Democrats charged that such publications represented a breach of security, Dulles argued that events since 1945 had rendered the agreements no longer secret. Public release of the Yalta Papers raked open old wounds. Democrats argued on the floor of Congress that these had been military, not political decisions, and Republicans refuted their claims. On the other hand, the episode resulted in another public relations triumph for the administration. In an April 1955 Gallup poll, nearly half of the public sampled believed the State Department had acted correctly in releasing the papers, while only 37 percent (mostly Democrats, of course) objected.

In the spring of 1955, largely due to the festering Formosa crisis, a number of Democrats launched a "peace offensive." Led by Senator George, they urged President Eisenhower to agree to a summit meeting with the Russians, a proposal strongly backed by the Western European Allies. In May, Eisenhower reluctantly agreed. The four-power summit was set for July 18, 1955, at Geneva. Major agenda items were to be arms control and what to do about the problem of divided Germany.

Eisenhower's decision to go to Geneva infuriated the GOP Old Guard. Styles Bridges stormed on the Senate floor that all such conferences produced "appeasement, compromise, and weakness," and Joseph McCarthy emerged from his postcensure obscurity to offer a vindictively inspired resolution requiring the president to discuss with the Russians "the present and future status of the nations of Eastern Europe." The ensuing debate was a brawl, with the Democrats, led by Lyndon Johnson and Walter George, posing as statesmanlike defenders of the administration's search for peace. The outcome disappointed both the Democrats and the most extremist Republicans. McCarthy's measure was defeated 77–4, with only Jenner, Langer, and Malone sticking with him. "The irony . . . ," observes Oshinsky, "was that McCarthy had united his party behind Dwight Eisenhower as it had never been united before."

The big news to come out of the Geneva summit was Eisenhower's "Open Skies" proposal—a suggestion that the Russians and the Americans agree to permit mutual aerial surveillance in order to reduce the escalating fears that fed the arms race. The Soviets did not agree to the proposal. In fact, the summit produced no positive conclusions, other than an accord on future cultural exchanges. Progress was made, however, toward the broad objective of improving the "spirit" of U.S.-Soviet diplomacy. Symbolized by pictures of a smiling Ike next to Soviet leaders Bulganin and Khrushchev, the "spirit of Geneva" dominated the American media in the aftermath of the summit.

The president held a lengthy briefing session for congressional leaders upon his return, assuring them that "there were no secret agreements made, nothing initialed, nothing signed." He felt confident in reporting that the Russians "understood the scope of modern war and the terrible consequences of fallout." In a televised address to the nation that same night, Eisenhower repeated this essentially hopeful message.

"The real significance of the conference," Divine contends, "was the evident realization by both sides that nuclear war was unthinkable." But, he adds, "[e]qually important was the emergence at Geneva of Dwight Eisenhower as the world's most eloquent spokesman for peace." There is no question that Eisenhower got political mileage out of this image at home. A Gallup poll held just after the Summit showed nearly 80 percent of the people thought the conference had produced gains. Moreover, the Democratic "peace offensive" discernible in the spring of 1955 was defused. But on the whole, no change had been wrought in the Cold War.

The "spirit of Geneva," however, had a positive influence on American life. Paralleling the changed diplomatic atmosphere was a new, more libertarian tendency in court opinions concerning sedition and the threat of subversion. "Even if there had been no censure battle" in December 1954, writes Oshinsky, "McCarthy's influence would have been severely curtailed by the easing of Cold War tensions at home and abroad."

Meanwhile, Eisenhower continued to enhance his powers through his use of the CIA as an operational arm of American foreign policy. Its funds and activities legally shielded from congressional oversight, the agency steadily expanded its sphere of operations in the mid-1950s. Initially, Eisenhower had based his protection of the agency on his general defense of executive authority against assaults by McCarthy, saying that he feared that an intelligence oversight committee in Congress would be controlled by the senator's supporters. But after McCarthy's fall, the president did not let down his guard. When Democrat Mike Mansfield moved in early 1955 to set up a CIA oversight committee, he encountered firm resistance from the administration. Eisenhower aided the agency's director, John Foster Dulles's brother, Allen Dulles, in the successful effort to block Mansfield's bill.

In early 1956, Eisenhower ensured periodic review of the government's intelligence activities by establishing an eight-member advisory committee, but this panel was a far cry from a congressional oversight committee. With the agency's U-2 overflight surveillance capabilities rapidly developing in 1955–1956, and its activities in remote trouble spots unhampered by congressional interference, Eisenhower enjoyed a powerful independence of action.

The Politics of Dead Center

The 1954 elections had produced the ambiguous situation of a highly popular president and a Congress controlled by the opposition. This situation had great impact on the outlook for domestic policy. On taxes, education, civil rights, resource policy, and farm policy, there ensued conflict, false starts, and irresolution. Eisenhower, believing that his continued personal popularity meant that his "mandate" of 1952 lived on, continued to press policies which the Democrats refused to accept.

In 1955, the nation was enjoying boom times. Production was up across the board, with the automobile industry leading the way, and consumer prices were rising only very slowly. The Democrats were interested in fostering further economic growth through a tax cut. Speaker Rayburn took the initiative, proposing to give every taxpayer a cut of $20 for each dependent. Eisenhower, deeply concerned about balancing the federal budget, warned that he would oppose Rayburn's bill. "[F]urther tax cuts will be possible," he announced in his 1955 State of the Union message, "when justified by lower expenditures and by revenue increases arising from the nation's economic growth." The tax reduction fight was brief and decisive. The president prevailed in the Senate, with the support of most of the southern Democrats. "We overstepped ourselves," remarked a Democratic party strategist, "trying to find an issue."

Shortly afterward, the Eisenhower administration experienced a major political embarrassment. In April 1955, Dr. Jonas Salk announced perfection of a vaccine that could prevent the dreaded infantile paralysis (polio)—a disease that had taken on epidemic proportions in the mid-fifties. In order to make Salk's three-injection series available to children in even the poorest families, Eisenhower secured from Congress over $30 million in grants for distribution of the vaccine. Health, Education and Welfare (HEW) Secretary Oveta Culp Hobby caused a public relations disaster, however, by voicing her conservative preference that the states should take responsibility for getting the vaccine to their citizens, and then by botching the federal distribution scheme. With demand for the Salk vaccine exceeding its availability and some children reportedly contracting polio from defective batches, Hobby's inept handling of the media only made matters worse. By July, she was gone. Her successor, Marion Folsom, proved more adept. Within a year the vaccine supply was equal to demand, and the incidence of infantile paralysis had fallen dramatically.

The polio vaccine crisis intensified Democratic charges that Eisenhower's policies were unresponsive to human needs. These accusations might have been blunted through passage of an administration proposal for federal aid to help meet the growing school shortage in the country, but the measure became ensnarled in the so-called Powell amendment. Proposed by Harlem (New York) Democrat Adam Clayton Powell as an addition to the school construction bill, the rider aimed to deny funds to any state continuing to segregate its schools. Neither the aid bill nor the Powell amendment got out of committee in 1955, but a year later the school aid package made it to the House floor, and the Powell amendment along with it. Northern Republicans, opposed on principle to federal aid for public schools, eagerly joined with liberals to tack the desegregation rider onto the measure; they then joined with disgruntled southerners and Catholics opposed to the proposal because it failed to include aid for parochial schools, to defeat the bill, 224–194.

Civil rights presented a thorny problem in the aftermath of the *Brown* decision. A year after its momentous May 1954 ruling, the Supreme Court issued a ruling known as *Brown II,* establishing procedures for implementing desegregation. Delegating the details to the local courts, the Court called for "all deliberate speed" in achieving results. The ruling was an invitation to obstructionists, and legislatures throughout Dixie hastily threw up laws establishing "freedom of choice" for parents and "pupil placement" schemes permitting circumvention of desegregation. Meanwhile, several Deep South states engaged in campaigns to roll back already low black voter registration.

At the local level, heretofore respectable whites banded together in White Citizen's Councils to block implementation of the Court's decision. "[I]n black belt areas," writes Numan Bartley in *The Rise of Massive Resistance: Race and Politics During the 1950's,* the council, "like the Ku Klux Klan thirty years before, was a bourgeois phenomenon. Its appeal . . . was to the middle class of the towns and villages. . . . As the organization spread into the cities, however, it tended to enlist the urban proletariat." Broad-based and varied in composition, the Citizens' Council movement enjoyed considerable political clout in the South. A number of prominent southern Democratic politicians encouraged the councils in their race baiting. Senator Eastland, for example, was a featured speaker at many council rallies, as were Strom Thurmond, Georgia Governor Marvin Griffin, and Representatives John Bell Williams of Mississippi and James C. Davis of Georgia.

The administration maintained a policy of noninterference in civil rights matters. Eisenhower pleaded for "restraint" on both sides, while the Justice Department declined to get involved on the basis that suits between private citizens and school boards were not public disputes. Predictably, the department resisted pressure from Powell and others to intervene against the arrests of young pastor Martin Luther King, Jr., and other blacks then boycotting the segregated bus system in Montgomery, Alabama.

Inside the administration, Brownell pushed the president to propose a moderate civil rights program emphasizing voting rights. But Eisenhower balked, believing that since his previous actions on behalf of desegregation had won him little support among blacks, new initiatives were not likely to help and would alienate the white South. Meanwhile, southern Democrats in Congress registered their opposition to desegregation by issuing the "Southern Manifesto." Signed by over eighty House members and all Dixie Senators except three with national ambitions (Johnson, Kefauver, and Gore), the manifesto pledged resistance "by all legal means" to the Supreme Court's *Brown* decree. Its issuance confirmed Eisenhower's belief that advocacy of civil rights legislation could be damaging in an election year. The administration sent a weak bill to the Hill in April, but it languished in the Senate Judiciary Committee.

Eisenhower also attempted to steer a moderate course through other sticky issue areas, including agriculture and resource policy. In 1954, the administration had secured passage of a farm bill including flexible rather than fixed price supports.

The extreme conservatism of Secretary of Agriculture Benson, however, had kept the "farm problem" alive. As a device to reduce surpluses that were keeping commodity prices low, in late 1955 Benson and Eisenhower came up with the idea for a "soil bank," which called for the government to pay farmers for taking land out of production and giving it over to ungrazed grass or forest. When Congress enacted the soil bank plan, but attached to it a series of rigid price support features, the president vetoed it. In late May 1956 Eisenhower signed a version he found more satisfactory. Despite this seeming victory, however, as Alton Lee has written in *Dwight D. Eisenhower: Soldier and Statesman,* "[t]he benefits of the soil bank never materialized. Farmers took the poorest land out of production, poured commercial fertilizers on the rest and surpluses persisted."

Resource development issues also posed significant problems for the administration, as Eisenhower attempted to defend his "partnership" strategy as a middle way between federal development and unfettered private enterprise. "Partnership," however, generally amounted to federal abdication of authority on issues of power and resources. The president and his controversial, sometimes tactless secretary of the interior, Douglas McKay, prevailed over Democratic efforts in Congress to enact a bill for a federally constructed high dam at Hells Canyon. In 1956, McKay was succeeded at Interior by Fred Seaton, a White House intimate with Nebraska roots. This switch proved a benefit to the administration. As Elmo Richardson observes in *Dams, Parks, and Politics,* Seaton's administrative skill and congenial personality permitted him to dampen controversy over power and resource issues even while maintaining the "partnership" approach. The new secretary's "undramatic but firm approach," writes Richardson, "and the greater confidence he received from the White House advisers enabled him to earn for the department the accolades of 'new look' and 'good bye giveaway.' "

On the question of natural gas deregulation, too, Eisenhower encountered political problems. This time, Eisenhower found himself compelled to veto his own bill when it reached his desk. The looming 1956 elections were a major consideration. After South Dakota Senator Francis Case reported that gas interests had tried to slip him $2,500 prior to the vote on the deregulation bill (which he then declined to support), Eisenhower felt he had to follow Case's example. Complaining to the Republican leaders about the "incredible stupidity of the industry," the president issued a sharply worded veto. "[G]iven that the Republican Party was counting on millions in contributions from the oil industry for the upcoming campaign," Stephen Ambrose has observed, "the veto was an act of some courage."

From another perspective, the veto of the natural gas bill was a concession to political necessity. Eisenhower had good reason to be sensitive to the integrity issue in early 1956. Several months before, a major flap had developed over the so-called Dixon-Yates affair. Two entrepreneurs, Edgar Dixon and Eugene Yates, had succeeded in negotiating a contract with the government to supply additional needed electric power to the Memphis area; this contractual agreement symbolized Eisenhower's "partnership" doctrine in that the Dixon-Yates facility represented an alternative to further expansion of the TVA. When it was revealed that the intermediary in the negotiations leading up to the contract was guilty of conflict of interest, the administration was placed in a very awkward position. Fortunately, the city of Memphis decided to build its own power plant, rendering the contract unnecessary. For the White House, however, Dixon-Yates remained a black mark. Adding to the administration's image problems was the case of Air Force Secretary Harold Talbott, who had been caught using his office for the benefit of his New York engineering firm. Talbott became such a liability that his resignation was accepted by the president in July 1955. For an administration already viewed as a coterie of millionaires, such publicity was very damaging.

All was not bleak for the administration, however. In 1956 occurred one of its greatest domestic policy triumphs, passage of the Interstate Highway Act. Described by Alton Lee as a "lasting monument of the 'partnership' concept," the Interstate Act was successfully pressed on Congress as a defense measure. Indeed Eisenhower, who was much impressed by the German *Autobahn* system, saw a federally assisted superhighway network as crucial to the nation's Cold War defense strategies. As enacted, the Interstate Act called for the federal government to pay 90 percent of the total costs (estimated at $31 billion), and the states, 10 percent, and provided for financing these costs through federal taxes on gasoline, tires, diesel fuel, and motor vehicles themselves.

The domestic policy battles of 1955 and 1956 were nettlesome to Eisenhower, but they were insignificant compared to the dark cloud that crossed the political horizon in late 1955. On September 24, while vacationing in Denver, the president suffered a coronary thrombosis. He stabilized quickly, and the government seemed to function well enough while he recuperated, but for a time there was serious doubt as to the president's political future. By December, however, Eisenhower seemed intent on running for reelection, confiding to Press Secretary Jim Hagerty that he was "appalled" at the lack of qualified Democrats.

In March 1956, Eisenhower announced his willingness to give another four years to his country. Not even another brief health setback three months later, when he underwent emergency surgery following a severe bout of ileitis, sidetracked him for long. It was not just that Eisenhower sought a referendum on his first four years, and perhaps an opportunity to complete what he had begun. As he admitted in a letter to his close friend Swede Hazlett, he felt "guilty ... that [he] had failed to bring forward and establish a logical successor." The implication about Vice President Nixon was clear: Eisenhower obviously had his doubts that Nixon was up to the top job.

Eisenhower Ascendant

The second half of 1956 was filled with drama and danger. If the inevitable rematch between Eisenhower and Adlai Stevenson promised more yawns than thrills, at least some interesting subplots surrounded the vice presidential nominations in both parties. The real action, however, was on the world stage, as tensions over the Suez Canal erupted into a brief war in the Middle East during the last weeks of the American presidential campaign. Simultaneously, seismic waves were generated behind the Iron Curtain by a revolt in Hungary. Never had there seemed better reasons to keep a steadying hand at the national helm than in November 1956. Eisenhower, already a shoo-in for reelection, benefited even further from the state of crisis.

As Stephen Ambrose has written, Eisenhower's selection of a running mate for his second term was "far more critical than it had been in 1952, not so much in terms of voter appeal, but in the possibility that the running mate might have to become the candidate, or succeed [him] upon his death." Perhaps that was why the preconvention period saw conspiratorial machinations, directed largely by administration disarmament adviser (and perennial White House aspirant) Harold Stassen, to dump Nixon from the ticket. Or perhaps it was just that Nixon, mistrusted and disliked by many as an opportunist in 1952, had not done enough to assuage such feelings in the intervening four years. It was correctly suspected that the president harbored feelings toward the vice president that were, at best, ambiguous. Though discreet in his public utterances, Eisenhower on several occasions disparaged Nixon within earshot of his intimates. Moreover, in December 1955, he had held a private talk with Nixon, offering the vice president virtually any cabinet post (except State or Justice) if he wished to leave the ticket. Nothing was decided at this private meeting, but Nixon's status was left uncertain. There is evidence also that Eisenhower dangled the second spot on the ticket before Robert Anderson, a Texan who had recently served as deputy secretary of defense and whom the president greatly admired. But Anderson was not interested, and Eisenhower remained silent on the subject of Nixon. It was not lost on the vice president that a single affirmative statement from Eisenhower could have ended the speculation once and for all.

In these propitious circumstances, Stassen schemed. On July 20, just four weeks before the GOP convention, Stassen, armed with poll data, visited Eisenhower to persuade him to drop Nixon. As a replacement, he suggested Governor Christian Herter of Massachusetts, a good but singularly colorless man, and a longtime internationalist who was certain to turn off much of the old Taft wing of the party. Three days after his visit, Stassen announced that Eisenhower had approved an open contest for the vice presidential nomination. Such was not to be, however. Whatever his private feelings—and whatever his motives in giving Stassen so long a leash—Eisenhower was brought back to political reality when Nixon was endorsed by nearly 90 percent of the 203 House Republicans. He continued to withhold unequivocal support for Nixon, but on the eve of the convention he coerced Stassen into agreeing to second Nixon's nomination. On August 22, the convention formally approved the Eisenhower-Nixon ticket. One thing about the flap over Nixon, Eisenhower confided to a friend in late July: "It did stir up some interest."

On the Democratic side, meanwhile, a brief race occurred between Stevenson, the odds-on favorite for the 1956 nomination, and Estes Kefauver. For a time in the fall of 1955, while Eisenhower lay ill in Denver, others had expressed interest in the nomination, notably Averell Harriman. Undoubtedly, only a heart attack he himself had suffered two months before the president's kept Senate Majority Leader Johnson out of the running. But Eisenhower's clear reentry into the 1956 picture swept the fainthearted from the field; only Kefauver hung in against Governor Stevenson. As in 1952, the Tennessean proved a fast starter on the campaign trail, winning an impressive victory in the New Hampshire primary against only token opposition, and then besting Stevenson in their first head-on contest in Minnesota. But Stevenson managed to defeat Kefauver in seven of the remaining primaries, including the crucial Florida and California contests. Kefauver withdrew in late July.

The drama in the Democratic party was not yet over,

however, as Stevenson faced a new challenge from Harriman, whose candidacy was supported by party liberals and former President Truman. Harriman's last-minute candidacy caused a flurry of excitement, but his hopes ended when the convention adopted the moderate platform plank on civil rights favored by the Stevenson forces, rather than a strong plank being pushed by dissident liberals. After taking the nomination on the first ballot, Stevenson surprised the delegates by leaving the choice of his running mate up to the convention. Though the glamorous young senator from Massachusetts, John Kennedy, came close to winning, in the end—despite feverish southern opposition—Kefauver won second place on the ticket.

Stevenson launched his campaign with the vision of a "New America," a call to battle that rekindled the enthusiasm of party liberals. But the former governor was in an uphill fight that he could not possibly win. Eisenhower, confident of victory, initially campaigned only in a limited way, leaving most of the task to Nixon. Finally, convinced by the Republican National Committee that a big victory could be crucial to his success in dealing with the new Congress, no matter which party controlled it, the president stepped up his efforts, and his criticisms of Stevenson became more acerbic.

A major reason for Eisenhower's increased activity was the nature of the campaign Stevenson chose to wage. Confronted by polls showing greater voter confidence in the Republicans on foreign policy, the Democratic standard bearer might have been wise to stay away from international and defense matters. But by September, he began to speak out against the draft and to emphasize the need for a nuclear test ban to counter the rising dangers from nuclear fallout and the proliferation of atomic capabilities. This represented a confusion, if not a reversal, of themes the Democrats had developed earlier. Thwarted on the "peace issue" by Eisenhower's summitry of 1955, party spokesmen had resumed sniping at the administration for failing to keep pace with Soviet firepower, especially after Soviet Premier Khrushchev had hinted at the imminent unveiling of a Soviet Intercontinental Ballistic

Missile (ICBM). Stevenson himself had even charged that the Eisenhower administration had been "dangerously dilatory" in meeting the Soviet challenge. His calls for a test ban in the presidential campaign therefore seemed strangely out of place.

To Eisenhower, they seemed a "design for disaster . . . ," and he said so. It did not help the Democrats when Russian leader Bulganin publicly announced his approval of "certain public figures in the United States" who were calling for a test ban. Stevenson, said Vice President Nixon, was nothing but a "clay pigeon" for the Soviets. The Democratic candidate's call for an end to the draft proved no more effective than his test-ban suggestions. A Gallup poll in early October 1956 showed that nearly three-fourths of the voters believed such a step premature.

In the final two weeks of the campaign, a most unusual thing happened. News of the presidential race was pushed from the headlines by events elsewhere—first in the Middle East, then in Eastern Europe. The chain of events resulting in crisis over the Suez Canal began in late July, when Egyptian leader Gamal Abdel Nasser nationalized that important waterway. Nasser's act was at least partially in retaliation for the Eisenhower administration's dangling of a huge loan before the Egyptians, only to withdraw it when Nasser appeared to be moving in a pro-Soviet direction. Now, with the British talking ominously about taking steps against Nasser, the president dispatched Secretary of State Dulles to London to urge restraint. This effort was futile. On October 29, Israel invaded Egypt, obviously with British approval. The next day, England and France together issued an ultimatum for a mutual withdrawal of the two sides to permit Anglo-French occupation and maintenance of the canal. The two western powers also vetoed a proposed Security Council resolution calling upon member nations to avoid the use of force in the Suez.

The three aggressor nations all felt confident that Eisenhower would support them, but the president surprised them. Acknowledging to Dulles that "it looks as if we're in for trouble," he speculated that he might have to use force to stop the allies in what he viewed as naked, opportunistic imperialism. "I will not under any circumstances," he told the secretary, "permit the fact of the forthcoming elections to influence my judgment."

Simultaneous with the threat of a general war in the Middle East, Soviet-dominated Eastern Europe erupted. In Poland, rioting and protests against Russian rule culminated in the return to power of nationalistic leader Wladyslaw Gomulka, and encouraged a similar uprising in Hungary. As increasingly severe rioting brought Soviet tanks and troops to Budapest, and the blood of Hungarian freedom fighters began to flow, Eisenhower resisted pressure from the CIA to intervene and avoided any appearance of abetting the revolutionaries. By the first of November, the Budapest rebels had been routed. The American response was limited to an announcement that 21,000 refugees would be accepted right away and legislation would be sought to allow for more.

The presidential election, its results preordained, seemed almost irrelevant to the main events. Eisenhower won a smashing reelection, carrying 57.3 percent of the popular vote and winning forty-one states totalling 457 electoral votes. All of these figures represented improvements over his landslide triumph of four years earlier.

The results also ensured that Eisenhower would continue to have to deal with a Democrat-led Congress. For the first time since Zachary Taylor was elected in 1848, the voters presented a newly elected president with a Congress in which his party controlled neither house. The Democrats picked up only two House seats and one Senate seat, but it was noteworthy that they made gains at all, given the magnitude of the president's victory. The Democratic majorities were 49–47 in the Senate, and 234–201 in the House. Among the most interesting results was Wayne Morse's defeat of former Interior Secretary Douglas McKay in the Oregon Senate race. New faces in the Senate included Republicans Jacob Javits of New York and Thruston Morton of Kentucky; Democratic freshmen of promise were Frank Church of Idaho, Joseph Clark of Pennsylvania, and Frank Lausche of Ohio.

It is relatively easy to explain such a lopsided outcome. Eisenhower's overwhelming popularity, combined with the international crises which seemed to require an experienced hand at the national helm, had simply made it impossible for Stevenson to win. But, within the overall results, some significant developments could be discerned. Civil rights, a prominent issue since the *Brown* decision, and certainly a factor in the Democratic nomination contest, wound up having only a minor impact. Both Stevenson and Eisenhower essentially reassured southern whites rather than aggressively pursuing the growing numbers of black voters. Eisenhower picked up the endorsement of the controversial Adam Clayton Powell, reportedly in exchange for protecting Powell against a possible investigation by the Internal Revenue Service. The president enjoyed increased support from black voters as a whole, improving upon his 1952 showing in several states where black voters made up significant shares of the population. These included Alabama, Arkansas, and North Carolina. He also registered slight gains among blacks in northern cities, including a 16.5 percent rise in Powell's Harlem district of New York City. Overall, however, Stevenson received more black votes than did Eisenhower.

Eisenhower also did well in the white South, adding Kentucky and Louisiana to the four southern states he had carried in 1952. But, as Herbert Parmet explains, civil rights was not the deciding issue. "Few southerners would agree," states Parmet, "that their solution [on civil rights] lay with embracing Eisenhower.... Still, there was the realization among conservatives, especially in the South, that their economic interests were more secure with the current administration than under any government dominated by northern liberals."

In fact, economic issues—particularly the fact of prosperity and the political evolution of an increasingly better-off working class—worked strongly to Eisenhower's benefit. Writes William Leuchtenburg in *In the Shadow of FDR,* "Many who had once supported Roosevelt had reached the conclusion that Eisenhower's 'modern Republicanism' suited an age of affluence better than FDR's depression-born ideology." This subtle shift in the self-identity of blue-collar voters is noted throughout the literature on electoral behavior in the 1950s, yet changes in the voting behavior of individual workers did not reflect diminution in the loyalty of organized labor as a whole to the Democratic party. Jimmy Hoffa and Dave Beck of the Teamsters Union were the only prominent labor leaders to endorse Eisenhower.

Television, an emergent force four years earlier, played a prominent part in the 1956 campaign. The number of sets in use had risen to 36 million, and politics was a popular attraction for viewers. It was estimated that up to 15 million households were tuned in to video coverage of a typical evening of the 1956 Democratic convention. To capitalize on the new medium's potential, both Eisenhower and Stevenson retained prestigious New York firms to handle their television advertising. The president probably benefited more than Stevenson. Not only was he supremely telegenic, but his handlers used the live camera to project an image of health and vigor, helping to relieve voters of concerns born of Ike's recent heart attack and intestinal surgery.

As the election campaign came to an end, the Suez crisis escalated. On November 5, following Anglo-French amphibious and paratroop assaults in the area of the Suez, Eisenhower dismissed a Soviet proposal for joint U.S.-Soviet military intervention against Israel, England, and France as "unthinkable," and warned darkly of the results of a Soviet strike. "[I]f those fellows start something," he said, "we may have to hit 'em—and, if necessary, with *everything* in the bucket."

Three days after his reelection, Eisenhower met with congressional leaders for a discussion of the dangerous world situation. Lyndon Johnson labeled the talk "very fruitful and helpful," and pledged that the Democrats would "not play politics with foreign policy." The next day, this message was countered by Jack Kennedy, who warned against "stifling"

party differences over foreign policy. Actual discord was min-
imal, however, as Eisenhower and Dulles pressured the French
and British into line in the Middle East by withholding American oil they desperately needed. By Christmas, French and
British troops had departed, to be supplanted by a United
Nations Emergency Force (UNEF) sent to oversee Egypt's reopening of the canal.

Israel, too, pulled back from the Sinai, but its insistence
on holding the citrus-rich Gaza Strip stymied efforts to get the
Suez reopened and gave Eisenhower political headaches through
the early months of 1957. With the threat of Soviet intervention viewed as a possibility, the president considered imposing
sanctions on the Israelis in order to force them to give up their
claims to the Gaza. But Democratic legislators, ever sensitive
to the important Jewish vote, would surely have reacted furiously against such a move. Finally, fearing punitive U.S.
action, Israel withdrew in mid-March.

Eisenhower's conduct during the Suez crisis has been the
subject of some argument among historians. Many have given
the president high marks for taking a stand against neocolonial
aggression by two of America's closest allies. Donald Neff, for
instance, has written (*Warriors at Suez: Eisenhower Takes
America into the Middle East*) that the president's "firm insistence that the rule of law be obeyed was one of the high
points of his presidency." On the other hand, the Suez crisis
marked the beginning of a serious decline of Western—including American—prestige and influence in the Middle East.
Moreover, the crisis severely strained the NATO alliance. In
Britain, Prime Minister Anthony Eden fell from power, though
Anglo-American relations seemed to emerge intact. France,
however, was another matter; already exhibiting a strong inclination to go their own way, after Suez the French seemed
a most unreliable ally.

Perhaps the most significant result of the Middle East
crisis was that Eisenhower and Dulles perceived a "power vac-
uum" in the region and proposed to fill it. In what was swiftly
dubbed the "Eisenhower Doctrine," the president asked Con-

gress in January 1957 for a sweeping area resolution similar to the one he had orchestrated two years earlier to deal with the Formosa crisis. This time, he sought not only authorization to intervene with force in the Middle East, if necessary, but also to send unspecified future military and economic aid to Arab nations that were imperiled by communism. This represented a fateful step. "[T]he striking feature of the Doctrine," Herman Finer has written (*Dulles Over Suez*), "was that America's own national interest was deemed to justify American armed intervention in the Middle East at America's exclusive direction."

Many Democrats objected to the proposed Middle East Resolution. Fiscal conservatives were critical because the measure included provisions for potentially costly foreign aid. Others, such as J. William Fulbright, raised constitutional issues. "It would not . . . ," said Fulbright, "be a proper discharge of our duty as Senators to give [the president] a blank check ahead of time and say, 'Whatever you did is all right.' " The administration relied on the strategy that had proved so successful in the case of the Formosa Resolution: it was up to Congress, Secretary of State Dulles said during closed hearings on the bill, "to decide whether or not they wish to respond, whether they prefer to take the responsibility of saying they know more about the conduct of foreign affairs than the President does."

The argument worked again. Though Eisenhower had to accept a significant change in wording (substituting for congressional "authorization" of possible future military force a declaration that the United States stood "prepared to use armed forces" if the situation warranted), the result was a significant victory for the president. It took two months, but the Middle East Resolution passed both houses with ease: 355–61 in the House, and 72–19 in the Senate. Southern conservatives were the most discernible block in opposition.

Eisenhower's position in the spring of 1957 was quite remarkable. The year just completed had been potentially devastating. Laid low by major emergency surgery at the age of sixty-five, he had quickly rebounded to full vigor. In an election that starkly revealed the continuing unpopularity of his party, he had won landslide reelection. And, perhaps most striking of all, several months of grave international crises that were at least partially attributable to his own policies left the president not weaker, but much stronger—celebrated worldwide as a peacemaker of principle, and clearly dominant over Congress in the decade-long battle for control over American foreign policy.

CHAPTER FOUR

Endings and Beginnings, 1957–1960

In the mid-1950s, when Dwight Eisenhower seemed at the height of his popularity and political influence, he repeatedly expressed two resolves. First, he wanted to ensure the loyalty of the Democratic majorities in Congress to the foreign policies of his administration. Second, he planned to recast his own party. In early 1954, he had remarked to Press Secretary James Hagerty on the need for "a word to put ahead of Republican—something like 'New' or 'Modern' or something." This objective required both recruiting attractive new candidates for the party and reshaping GOP policies to appeal to young voters.

As it turned out, neither of these two resolves bore results. Faced with a Democratic-controlled Congress throughout his second term, Eisenhower adhered to the formalities of bipartisan cooperation in setting the broad outlines of foreign policy, but more often he worked successfully to circumvent congressional authority. Meanwhile, serious new challenges abroad—ranging from war scares in Asia and the Middle East to the surprise Soviet launching of a space satellite that transformed and intensified the arms race—stiffened Democratic resistance to whatever bipartisan cooperation may have been possible.

As for Eisenhower's goal of remaking the Republican party, such an overhaul never occurred. Despite wishful thinking by liberal-minded administration figures, who wrote about Eisenhower's commitment to reforming the GOP (for instance, Arthur Larson, in *A Republican Looks at his Party,* and Emmet J. Hughes, in *The Ordeal of Power*), the president showed no sustained enthusiasm for the project. In his second term, in fact, his conservatism on domestic matters seemed to increase. By the late 1950s, the Republican party, which his election and reelection were supposed to have revitalized, embraced many of the same positions it had held ten years earlier. By the end of the decade, the supposed political equilibrium of the Eisenhower years had dissolved. Events of the 1960s would demonstrate how far the nation was from solving its basic problems.

The Continuing Problem of Civil Rights

The era of stability and harmony seemingly heralded by Eisenhower's reelection did not last long. Almost immediately, the chronic problem of civil rights erupted once again. Despite occasional periods of remission and efforts by politicians in both parties to make it go away, the difficult challenge of defining the position of blacks in American society was to complicate political life through the rest of the Eisenhower years and for a decade beyond.

In 1956, election-year wariness in both parties had stalled action on a weak administration-sponsored civil rights bill. GOP gains among black voters in the fall produced a new dynamic as the Eighty-fifth Congress convened in 1957. Pro-civil rights forces in the administration, led by Brownell, now renewed their efforts to secure a voting rights enforcement bill. In the Democratic party, meanwhile, liberals—disenchanted by the failed policy of moderation followed by Stevenson and the congressional leadership—were determined to act. In late November, just days after the election, Senators Douglas, Humphrey, Pat McNamara, Morse, James Murray, and Richard Neuberger sent to all senators and senators-elect a "Democratic Declaration": a sixteen-point program with civil rights at the top of the list. Simultaneously, party chairman Paul Butler, an outspoken supporter of civil rights activism, worked with party liberals to establish the Democratic Advisory Committee (DAC), whose function would be to stake out a program for the party as a whole. Many moderates were now ready to cooperate with the liberals, for pragmatic reasons if for no other.

The administration's 1957 proposal was similar to that presented a year earlier. As drafted, it would create both an executive Commission on Civil Rights and a new Division of Civil Rights in the Justice Department, authorize the president to use troops to enforce civil rights laws, empower the attorney general to initiate civil action in instances where citizens had been denied the right to vote, and allow a judge to decide whether a jury would try a defendant in a criminal contempt case arising from a civil rights infraction. Most controversial from the outset were the provisions authorizing the attorney general to bring suit and the president to use troops (Part III), and the question of when jury trials should be granted to defendants in civil rights cases.

Eventual passage of the 1957 Civil Rights Act was due in part to Eisenhower's willingness to make major concessions, a willingness that reflected his lack of enthusiasm for the more ambitious portions of the bill. Also important was the role of Lyndon Johnson, who had decided that his presidential chances would be advanced by gaining credit for moderate civil rights measures. To "emancipate himself from the Confederate yoke," as Rowland Evans and Robert Novak have written in *Lyndon B. Johnson: The Exercise of Power,* the majority leader needed "to transform the Eisenhower bill into the Johnson bill." He began by corralling enough votes from moderate Democrats and Republicans to bypass Eastland's Judiciary Committee and bring the House-passed bill directly to the floor on June 20.

In addition to personal ambition, Johnson was driven by a realization that the Democratic party could be split, perhaps irrevocably, unless a compromise could be found. Two key amendments soon emerged: the Anderson-Aiken amendment struck from the bill the controversial Part III, while the O'Mahoney-Kefauver-Church amendment provided for jury trials in criminal contempt cases arising out of civil rights legislation. Eisenhower strongly opposed the jury-trial amendment, on the grounds that contempt was "a matter of fact," not "a matter of law." But Johnson prevailed, and on August 2, 1957, the Senate adopted the O'Mahoney-Kefauver-Church rider by a vote of 51–42; it then approved the full bill by 72–18 on August 7.

Nearly four weeks later, after further revision of the jury-trial amendment during the House-Senate conference, the bill was finally agreed to by both houses. Ultimately, the only votes cast against the bill in either chamber came from Deep South Democrats, but in fact the measure as enacted was more disappointing to liberals than to southerners. Eisenhower, urged by some black leaders to withhold his signature from so weak a measure, reluctantly signed it into law on September 9.

Eisenhower had all along stressed the voting rights sections of the 1957 bill. So, too, had Lyndon Johnson, in defending the measure to his constituents. The symbolic unleashing of the southern black vote was one of the most important results of the new law. Black registration in the eleven southern states, which had grown by almost 25 percent between 1952 and 1956, now seemed likely to increase dramatically, perhaps holding the key to a new political alignment in the South and nationally. This perception led many, especially the more activist Democrats, to consider taking further action on civil rights, since anticipated losses among southern whites might now be balanced by gains among newly enfranchised blacks.

From Eisenhower's perspective, the Civil Rights Commission established by the 1957 law also proved valuable. A bipartisan, six-member body, it would be left to drift by the administration, which viewed it, according to James Duram (*A Moderate Among Extremists*), as "a buffer which would absorb much of the shock, controversy, and criticism in the civil rights realm." Burk agrees with Duram's judgment of the commission, noting that its limited activities in the area of voting rights, school desegregation, and housing policy "helped free the administration from the necessity of issuing its own public pronouncements against Southern discrimination."

The ink had barely dried on the civil rights law when a major racial crisis exploded at Central High School in Little Rock, Arkansas. Some observers have suggested that the apparent southern victory in the fight over the jury-trial amendment in July and August of 1957 may have encouraged Arkansas Governor Orval Faubus to defy the two-year-old court order for school desegregation, but this seems a simplistic explanation. The Citizens' Councils and other segregationist elements in the South had been engaging in massive resistance since the *Brown II* ruling. When in the fall of 1956 Texas Governor Allan Shivers had interposed the state militia to block desegregation in the Texas towns of Mansfield and Texarkana, President Eisenhower had done nothing. White House inaction, more than anything else, gave Faubus confidence to act.

The confrontation in Little Rock began on September 2, when Faubus sent the Arkansas National Guard to block the doors of the high school, while a white mob milled threateningly in the streets. Twelve days later, Eisenhower met with the governor to persuade him to remove the guardsmen. The meeting left Eisenhower with the impression that the troops would be withdrawn, but Faubus—if indeed he ever intended to back down—changed his mind and held fast. As the administration pondered its next step, the Democratic Advisory Committee issued a statement on September 15, charging that Eisenhower had "failed in his duty to make the principle clear to all of the country that the first responsibility of a Governor is to uphold the Federal Constitution . . . ," and had "lost an

opportunity to exert leadership in behalf of law and order."
The DAC statement, of course, emphasized the North-South
rift in the Democratic party, as well as causing the administration discomfort.

On September 24, 1957, Eisenhower acted. Explaining his
decision to a nationwide radio and television audience that
evening, by executive order he federalized the Arkansas National Guard and dispatched to the scene 1,000 paratroopers
of the 101st Airborne Division. Insisting on a fine distinction
that escaped most southern listeners, the president said that
the federal troops were not "relieving" state and local authorities of their responsibilities, but were in Little Rock to
prevent interference with the court order. Invoking the spirit
of the Cold War, he observed that the Communists were no
doubt "gloating over this incident."

The reaction of leading southerners was quick, predictable, and vehement. Senator Russell, who earlier had been
asked by Faubus to represent him in court if Faubus were cited,
compared the president's action to Hitler's use of the Storm
Troopers. Russell's Georgia Senate colleague, Herman Tal-
madge, drew an analogy to the Soviets' use of tanks and troops
to destroy Hungarian sovereignty a year earlier. Others also
spoke out, including Senators Eastland, Olin Johnston of South
Carolina, and Lyndon Johnson (hedging against conservative
resentment of his role in the enactment of the Civil Rights Act
earlier in the year). The president met with a group of moderate
southern governors on October 2, and secured their help in
trying to negotiate with Faubus. No compromise was forthcoming, but tensions in Little Rock subsided sufficiently for
Eisenhower to withdraw half the troops by mid-October, and
the remaining forces by late November. The federalized
guardsmen remained in place, keeping an uneasy peace for the
rest of the school year.

Historians tend to agree about Eisenhower's intervention
in Little Rock. His primary motivation was to execute the law
of the land, but he also acted out of anger at what he considered
to be Faubus's treachery. According to Burk, Eisenhower's

"sense of having been betrayed by . . . Faubus, encouraged an action otherwise out of character with [his] political instincts." Although convinced that he was acting correctly, Eisenhower was uncomfortable serving as the champion of integration in Little Rock. He was, in the words of James Duram, "forced by events beyond his control to exercise his presidential powers in a way that he abhorred because of his determination to uphold his oath of office." Duram concludes: "It is not a story of the surrender of his moderation but rather its frustration."

Despite Eisenhower's use of troops, massive resistance dragged on, especially in Arkansas and Virginia. In Little Rock, the federalized national guard kept the desegregated schools open through the 1957–1958 school year, but Faubus succeeded in closing them for the entire following year while matters remained tied up in the courts. Finally, in September 1959, the city's schools reopened permanently. In Virginia, nine school districts that had attempted to comply with the desegregation order were closed down in 1958. Eisenhower temporized in the face of this challenge, remarking in one press conference that he "got very annoyed at the refusal of the North to see how deeply the people of the South feel about the integration issue."

In January 1959, the Supreme Court ruled Virginia's selective closings to be in violation of the equal protection clause of the Fourteenth Amendment, but no Little Rock-style clash was necessary. Southern business leaders and other influentials had begun to realize that school closings might make their states less attractive to corporations and other economic enterprises looking for places to locate, and played a critical role in bringing massive resistance to an end. By 1960, only three states in the Deep South (Alabama, Mississippi, and South Carolina) were still holding out against desegregation.

One political spin-off from Little Rock and from the massive resistance struggle as a whole was the launching of a brief but bitter vendetta against the Supreme Court by a formidable congressional bloc. Put off by decisions by the Warren Court that seemed to expand the bounds of permissible political dissent and to broaden federal authority in a number of areas, southern Democrats and conservative Republicans only narrowly failed in their efforts to limit the authority of the high bench.

The Little Rock confrontation had at least two other specific political repercussions. One was the collapse of the Republicans' "Operation Dixie," an ambitious plan to rebuild the GOP in the southern states. A second by-product benefited the Democrats more directly: the widening North-South rift in the party was closed by the president's decision to send troops into Little Rock. With southern segregationists focusing their resentment exclusively on the administration, and liberal Democrats no longer seen as exclusive champions of black civil rights, tensions within the party receded. The Democrats were thus well positioned in the last months of 1957 to make partisan hay out of the Russians' surprise launching of a small satellite named *Sputnik.*

Hard Times at Home and Abroad

Still smarting from his overwhelming defeat less than two weeks earlier, Adlai Stevenson observed to John Sparkman in November 1956: "I really don't believe Eisenhower would have been too hard to beat if he had been chopped up a little beforehand." That view was obviously reflected in the formation of the Democratic Advisory Committee, which was established to give the party a permanent unified voice on all issues, including foreign policy. Though the party's congressional leadership, notably including Johnson and Rayburn, opposed establishment of the DAC (and refused to join it) because they saw it as usurping their roles as spokesmen, the new panel got off a number of effective volleys against administration policy during the remainder of Eisenhower's presidency.

Throughout 1957, the most promising target for Democratic attack was administration defense policy, and in particular the missile development program. Building on a similar assault on a supposed "bomber gap" they had mounted several months earlier, defense-minded Democrats, led by Senators Stuart Symington and Henry Jackson, began to warn in spring 1957 that the United States was falling dangerously behind the Soviets in development of missiles. Symington charged that the Russians led in the production of all important military wares except surface missiles, and that the administration was purposely deceiving the American public about the situation.

CIA surveillance overflights of Soviet installations by the high-flying U-2, a program approved by President Eisenhower in 1956, produced evidence of Soviet missile development. Still, the administration and most of the American press maintained that the United States was at least even in the missile race, if not ahead. Eisenhower was sufficiently confident of this that in May 1957 he told a group of GOP congressional leaders that he regretted going along with as large an appropriation as he had for Project Vanguard, an undertaking designed to put a man-made satellite into orbit.

This official serenity was shattered by the Soviets' surprise announcement on October 4, 1957, that they had orbited a small satellite, *Sputnik.* Within a month, that triumph was followed by another, larger *Sputnik II* (with a live dog aboard) that had required a rocket thrust capability greater than that possessed by the United States. The administration's response to the initial Soviet announcement sounded defensive. Worst of all was Sherman Adams's flippant dismissal of the furor as an "outer-space basketball game." Both Eisenhower and Nixon were soon at pains to stress the scientific importance of the two *Sputniks,* with the president delivering a sobering radio and television address on the subject four days after the second Soviet launching. In his speech, Eisenhower balanced admiration for the scientific feat with calm insistence that Americans should not assume the nation was losing the Cold War. "So far as the satellite itself is concerned," he remarked in an October press conference, "that does not raise my apprehension, not one iota."

Democrats who had been stressing the issue of a "defense gap" now escalated their attack. "The storm," observed *Time,* "showed promise of being the most serious that Dwight Eisenhower [has] ever faced." The president used all means of persuasion on Symington, Jackson, Johnson, and other opposition leaders, including the suggestion that the Democrats themselves could wind up with a hefty share of the blame for any "gap," since Truman had spent practically nothing on missile development. Nothing helped, as the Democrats' genuine apprehensions were reinforced by their instinct to go for the political jugular. One who saw special opportunity was John Kennedy, whose stump-speaking on the "missile gap" was reported by *Time* in appropriate metaphor: "Orbiting around the U.S. last week, his targets marked, his re-entry problem possibly solved, was Massachusetts's rumple-haired Democratic Senator. . . . Ultimate destination (according to the easily de-coded Kennedy beeps): the White House."

Some Democrats revived Symington's earlier charges of secrecy and deception. A critical statement issued by the DAC in mid-October, for example, charged the administration with "unnecessary and excessive secrecy" and with "leading the people to believe that we have a national security which in fact we are rapidly losing." Many conservative Republicans also joined in the general call for an end to complacency. "The time has clearly come," pronounced Old Guard elder statesman Styles Bridges, "to be less concerned with the depth of pile on the new broadloom rug or the height of the tail fin on the new car and to be more prepared to shed blood, sweat and tears."

The press fanned public concern, particularly those organs, such as the *New York Times,* that had already been critical of Eisenhower's defense policies. Perhaps the most dramatic and widely read of the spate of articles that appeared on the subject in the last weeks of 1957 was Stewart Alsop's article, "How Can We Catch Up?" which appeared in the December 14 issue of the popular *Saturday Evening Post.* Overall, as Richard Aliano has described in *American Defense Policy from Eisenhower to Kennedy,* the media served a number of important functions for detractors of the administration in the partisan confrontation following *Sputnik:*

(1) it provided legislators with general information on the actions and views of those involved in the controversy; (2) it gave Congressional critics of administration policy intelligence on dissension within the executive branch; (3) it supplied "documentation" or "proof" which could be used to buttress the arguments of those opposed to the administration.

Sputnik had immediate political impact. In early October, Eisenhower announced the appointment of MIT President James Killian to the new position of special White House assistant for science and technology, an advisory position that was to carry significant responsibilities for the rest of Eisenhower's term in office. At the same time, the president made clear to his cabinet that any prospect of a tax cut for fiscal 1959 was ended, and that the administration must be ready to oppose any such proposal. The bad publicity given to interservice rivalry as a cause for delay in U.S. missile development also strengthened Eisenhower's commitment to secure a major reorganization of the Department of Defense. In 1958, Congress passed a sweeping reform bill that subordinated the separate branches to a civilian secretary. *Sputnik* also affected Pentagon planning. At the regular White House meeting for legislative leaders on December 3, 1957, presentations were given by new Secretary of Defense Neil McElroy and JCS Chief General Nathan Twining detailing a reassessment of the fiscal year 1959 defense program. McElroy assured the leaders that "a number of high priority projects were added to the program previously developed," with "marginal items" being dropped. The result, warned the secretary, was a budget "somewhat higher" than the year before.

But Eisenhower would not be stampeded into what he regarded as overreaction. This was evident in his handling of the Gaither Report at the end of 1957. A panel headed by Ford Foundation chairman H. Rowan Gaither had been appointed by the president to examine the question of how the nation might provide for civil defense if it experienced a nuclear attack. Just prior to news of *Sputnik,* the panel brought to the National Security Council a wide-ranging report presenting a bleak comparison of U.S. and Soviet defense capabilities. The panel observed that, unless trends were reversed, by 1959 the Soviets might be able to wipe out the United States with a single strike. When, inevitably, the secret report was leaked to the press, "missile gap" critics in the Democratic party seized on it as exhibit A. Eisenhower refused Lyndon Johnson's request for release of the full text. As in the Army-McCarthy hearings, the president cited executive privilege, arguing that advisory panels gave counsel "with the understanding that their advice will be kept confidential." Not until 1973 did the Gaither Report become public. Its specific contents surprised no one. Perhaps even more important than Eisenhower's refusal to release the report to Congress, however, was his refusal to follow its recommendations. "Only Ike could have gotten away with saying no," concludes Ambrose. "It was one of his finest hours."

In the midst of the clamor over *Sputnik,* Eisenhower was felled again by sudden illness—this time a stroke, on November 26, 1957. Rebounding quickly, he suffered no permanent effects other than a slight speech impairment, which gave to his subsequent public utterances a sometimes confused, or at least confusing, quality. Almost before the politicians and public could mull over the possibilities of Nixon assuming the presidency, Eisenhower was back in full command. The strength of his basic constitution was never more obvious.

The defense issue was kept alive through the winter of 1957–1958 by a special Senate Preparedness Subcommittee chaired by Lyndon Johnson. Clearly a vehicle for LBJ's White House aspirations, the panel heard a succession of experts, all of them, according to Aliano, "reinforcing the crisis-like atmosphere." The final report of the subcommittee was unanimously supported by both parties. Although the document was milder than Symington and some others had wanted, Democratic liberals were concerned that the party was assuming an irreversibly hawkish posture. An exchange of letters between Senators Morse and Lehman reflected this concern. Referring to the views of Johnson, Symington, Richard Russell, and others of their ilk as "chilling," Morse expressed a fear that "the Democratic Party was being entrapped." Replied Lehman: "Like you, I am deeply concerned. . . . We must convince people that the Democratic Party is not a war party." This major difference of opinion in the party would continue to haunt it not only through the 1960 election, but into the years of the Vietnam War.

Grudgingly, Eisenhower supported increases in defense spending in 1958. As a concession to political practicalities, he also decided to pursue development of soon-to-be-obsolete liquid-fuel missiles as well as solid-fuel projectiles. The "missile gap" issue would not subside, however, periodically gaining intensity in the months preceding the presidential election year of 1960. Still, Eisenhower held firm, more interested in reducing overall federal spending levels than in pandering to the purveyors of a "gap" he knew to be nonexistent because of the reports from regular and frequent U-2 overflights.

The "missile gap" was later conceded by the Eisenhower administration's Democratic successors to be a fiction. How sincerely Eisenhower's critics believed in its existence at the time may never be known. In any event, the president was able to keep public paranoia under control, even if he could not make the issue disappear. By mid-1958, the 25 percent of the electorate that felt Soviet scientists were ahead of their American counterparts had shrunk to 8 percent. The successful launching of three American satellites in late 1958 helped further to reduce public apprehensions.

In addition to defense reorganization, two other important pieces of legislation were proposed by the administration and passed by Congress in 1958 as a direct result of concerns born of *Sputnik*. The first was a law, proposed with some reluctance by Eisenhower, to place the missile and space exploration programs under a single civilian authority, the National Aeronautics and Space Administration (NASA). Simultaneously, both houses of Congress established permanent committees with oversight responsibilities in such matters.

The second *Sputnik*-inspired measure was the National Defense Education Act (NDEA). On the whole, it followed Eisenhower's January 1958 requests, including a large increase in scientific education funds for the National Science Foundation; federal grants for the improvement of testing, guidance, and counseling; additional funds for the hiring of math and science teachers; and support for graduate study in a number of security-related academic fields. As an aid-to-education bill, NDEA had been vulnerable to the same forces that had killed the administration's earlier school construction proposals. The difference in the final vote on the two (NDEA passed by 233–140 in the House and 62–26 in the Senate) was the support of southerners, as Adam Clayton Powell and his supporters had cooperated with Eisenhower by not appending a desegregation rider to the 1958 bill. The National Defense Education Act was a historic milestone—as James Sundquist has pointed out, "not so much because of the specific provisions . . . but because of the psychological breakthroughs it embodied."

While the political pot simmered at home, Eisenhower successfully handled two explosive situations abroad, in each case drawing upon the special authority granted to him in advance by the Congress. In mid-July 1958, he sent fourteen thousand American troops into Lebanon in order to bolster the endangered prowestern government of Camille Chamoun. By late October, the Lebanese crisis had abated; Chamoun's government had survived, the American troops had departed, and the first major implementation of the "Eisenhower Doctrine" was acknowledged a general success. Leading Democrats, including Speaker Rayburn and Senator Fulbright, had been unenthusiastic when Eisenhower proposed intervention in Lebanon, but in the end the president faced little partisan criticism for his action.

The second international crisis of 1958, the resumption of shelling of Quemoy and Matsu by the People's Republic of China (PRC), became a hotter partisan issue than the intervention in Lebanon. Ultimately, Eisenhower's response to the PRC's shelling of the islands was limited to providing naval protection so that Chiang Kai-shek could supply his troops in Quemoy, and sending the Nationalist leader a number of sidewinder air-to-air missiles. The PRC's shelling was an old problem fraught with greater dangers than ever because of increased Soviet military capabilities. In the circumstances, writes Robert Divine in *Eisenhower and the Cold War*, "Eisenhower decided that the wisest course of action was to do what he had done in 1955—'Keep the Communists guessing.' "

The president's ambiguous stance kept the politicians and the public guessing as well. While the "China lobby" warned against appeasement of the PRC, Democratic leaders were divided and somewhat hesitant in their criticisms. Most who spoke out cautioned Eisenhower against taking too much power into his own hands in dealing with the Formosa crisis. Senate Foreign Relations Committee chairman Theodore Francis Green (Rhode Island) and Wayne Morse both insisted that it had been understood when the treaty with Nationalist China and the Formosa Resolution were approved, that American troops would not be employed in the area without specific congressional approval. Stevenson advocated a cease-fire and charged that U.S. actions were "actually creating sympathy for Red China and misgivings about our good sense."

Armed with knowledge from U-2 overflights that the Chinese Communists were not mobilizing for an invasion, Eisenhower stuck to his policy of tough talk coupled with vague threats. "[A] Western Pacific 'Munich' would not buy us peace or security," he insisted. On October 6, the PRC announced a one-week suspension of the shelling. Though no one could be certain at the time, this actually marked the end of the crisis. Eventually, the mainland Chinese settled on an absurd strategy of a preannounced every-other-day bombardment of Quemoy and Matsu. "And so the crisis was permitted to peter out," writes Herbert Parmet, "without any final solution."

Eisenhower's success in dealing with the "second Formosa crisis" ensured continued public confidence in his handling of international problems, but the 1958 off-year elections threatened to be very bad for Republicans generally. The civil rights issue and the appeal of the Democrats' "missile gap" charges were part of the reason, but clearly most troublesome of all for the Republicans was the unhealthy state of the economy. By late 1958, a downturn that had begun the year before had deepened into persistent recession, particularly affecting workers in heavy industry and midwestern farmers. Much-publicized battles within the GOP, at times pitting congressional conservatives against the White House and, on one occasion, even seeming to set Eisenhower and his treasury secretary at odds, projected an image of irresolution and identified the party more with the goal of balancing the budget than with reducing unemployment and public suffering. Eisenhower's vetoes of bills for public works and area redevelopment only reinforced such an image. Meanwhile, Democratic congressional leaders, sniffing political blood, did their utmost to blame the president's party for the hard times. Rejecting a plea by northern and western Democrats to lend a hand in trying to enact a tax cut in 1958 to stimulate the slumping economy, Speaker Rayburn stated with candor: "I can't put the Democratic Party's neck in a noose. . . . It is no part of the congress's duty to take Ike off the hook. If they won't move first, let them take the rap; let them answer for the recession in November."

Answer they did. By October, the economy began a slow recovery, but its effects were not yet sufficiently in evidence to help the GOP in the elections. Also damaging was the continuing unpopularity of conservative Secretary of Agriculture Ezra Taft Benson with farmers, an antagonism exacerbated by Eisenhower's 1958 veto of a Democratic-sponsored bill to maintain high agricultural price supports. Not surprisingly, the Republicans lost a total of eighteen House seats in the agricultural heartland states. In addition, the GOP suffered in states where the antiunion "right-to-work" issue surfaced, including especially the important states of California and Ohio. In the Golden State, the Senate seat vacated by Knowland (who was defeated in the gubernatorial election) was lost to the Democrats, and in Ohio, John Bricker was beaten. In these two states alone, the GOP lost a total of six House seats. Bricker's loss, together with the death of Joe McCarthy in 1957, the retirements of Edward Martin and William Jenner, and the electoral defeats of George (Molly) Malone and Herman Welker, meant that the conservative "class of 1946" was entirely gone from the Senate. As David Reinhard notes in *The Republican Right Since 1945,* "the Old Guard was dead, and the term itself was seldom used after 1958."

Polls in late 1958 showed that race relations and civil rights actually outranked unemployment as a public concern, even if they were less significant forces in the election than economic issues. Clearly, moderation on race had produced some important victories within the Democratic party in 1958: the successes of Albert Gore and newcomer Ralph Yarborough in the Tennessee and Texas Senate races, respectively, reflected voter rejection of extreme segregationist appeals. Nationally, *Congressional Quarterly* tabulated that the 1958 elections increased the ranks of civil rights supporters by at least six in the Senate, and twelve in the House.

The overall results of the 1958 election were devastating to the GOP. The Senate shifted from a narrow 49–47 Democratic majority to a whopping 64–34, while the House moved from a 234–201 Democratic advantage to 282–154. In addition, the Republicans lost seven governorships, holding only fourteen after the debris of the elections was cleared away. Researchers found evidence of "massive" defections, especially among "weak" Republican party identifiers, nearly half of whom deserted the party in 1958.

Eisenhower, writes Ambrose, was unconcerned with these results because of "his faith in his informal alliance with the southern Democrats." Indeed, many members of the Republican National Committee, meeting at Des Moines in January 1959, blamed the president's inattention for the debacle. This interpretation does not hold up, however. After campaigning stridently against Democratic "extremists" and "radicals," Eisenhower was uncharacteristically vitriolic in his press conference the morning after the election. Expressing amazement that only two years after his landslide reelection, the voters had effected "a complete reversal" by voting for a lot of "world class" spenders, he said he could "not see where there is anything that these people consciously want the administration to do differently." His solution? ". . . I promise this: for the next two years, the Lord sparing me, I am going to fight this as hard as I know how."

National Security and Party Politics

Much was different in the last two years of Eisenhower's presidency. Most obviously, the cast of characters had changed. In September 1958, chief White House assistant Sherman Adams, long the bane of Republicans and Democrats alike in their quest for access to the president, was forced to resign under a barrage of uncontested allegations that he had exchanged favors for expensive gifts from an old friend, industrialist Bernard Goldfine. Adams saw nothing wrong in his actions, and indeed his conduct may not have been out of the ordinary for the time. But for an administration that, in the wake of the Truman scandals, had pledged to be "clean as a hound's tooth," the issue posed a major problem, and Adams had to go. Predictably, he proved irreplaceable in the Eisenhower White House.

The cabinet had also changed dramatically. Gone were original team members Herbert Brownell, George Humphrey, Douglas McKay, and Oveta Culp Hobby. The strongest pillar of all crumbled soon after, as John Foster Dulles, gravely ill with a cancer that would kill him a month later, resigned in April 1959. In general, the replacements were able. Robert Anderson at Treasury and Fred Seaton at Interior probably represented improvements, and William Rogers at Justice and Arthur Flemming at HEW were highly competent. But Brownell and Humphrey had been sources of personal support to Eisenhower, and the loss of Dulles was devastating to him. Dulles's replacement at State was the kindly but fragile Christian Herter, who was no more than a caretaker. Without doubt, the recast administration lacked the dynamic potential of Eisenhower's first term.

Worsening the problem were the huge, aggressive Democratic majorities in the House and Senate. The leadership remained nominally the same—Johnson in the Senate and Rayburn in the House. But liberal ranks had swelled in both chambers, including a number of high-energy, able Senate freshmen. These differences in personnel combined to produce a major shift in the political atmosphere in 1959–1960. No longer was the president in control, as he had managed to be even in the face of Democratic congressional majorities from 1955 through 1958. The last two years Eisenhower spent in the White House saw him constantly on the defensive, as Congress criticized and scrutinized the operations of the CIA and the direction of American foreign policy, and as Democrats constructed their own domestic policy agenda.

To this point, Eisenhower had enjoyed a fairly free hand in his use of the national security machinery that had existed since the early days of the Cold War. The virtual autonomy enabled the administration to engineer the successful CIA-assisted coups in Iran and Guatemala, and to develop and put into operation the U-2 surveillance planes. His reliance on the NSC meant also that most major foreign policy formulation was a *fait accompli* by the time congressional leaders learned of it. *Sputnik* and the ensuing "missile gap" controversy had begun to undermine this arrangement, however. After the 1958 elections congressional Democrats grew bolder, conducting major inquiries into the operations of both the NSC and the CIA.

Whereas Truman had put the NSC to use only sporadically, Eisenhower institutionalized it as an important part of the policy-making process. The council met regularly, on Thursday mornings, usually with more than twenty attendees, and it advised Eisenhower on the most sensitive and crucial issues. In the weeks immediately following *Sputnik,* Senator Fulbright had tried to interest Lyndon Johnson in giving a green light to a Foreign Relations Committee probe of the NSC, but Johnson—who had already announced the beginning of "a searching inquiry" of the missile program by his Preparedness Subcommittee—did not encourage Fulbright.

In early 1959, Henry Jackson, a member of the Senate Government Operations Committee, renewed the idea. In a major speech at the National War College, he criticized existing policy-making methods, saying that they were not producing "clearly defined and purposeful strategy" for victory in the Cold War. Jackson then announced that his committee was planning a full-scale inquiry into the NSC. Eisenhower tried to kill the investigation by writing an open letter to Johnson, arguing that the probe "would inescapably thrust Congressional investigative activities deeply into the Nation's highest national security and foreign policy deliberative processes which traditionally as well as Constitutionally have remained within the province of the Chief Executive." The result, the president warned, would be "needless controversy" that might "inhibit and constrict" the nation's ability to act in world affairs.

The president's efforts did not succeed. In mid-July, the Senate approved $60,000 for purposes of conducting the NSC study, and shortly afterward Jackson was named to head the subcommittee. Eisenhower backed down with grace, pledging cooperation on the understanding that the study would be "directed to procedures and machinery, and not to substance." The hearings lasted into the succeeding Congress and no report was issued until Eisenhower had left the White House, but the Senate's insistence on carrying through its intentions, in the face of strong opposition from the president, accurately reflected the new political balance.

The CIA, too, came under sharper scrutiny, as critics of the agency's operations got another opportunity in the spring of 1960 to exercise stronger oversight. The precipitating incident was public disclosure by the Soviets on May 5 that they had shot down one of the CIA's U-2 reconnaissance planes over Soviet territory. Eisenhower, aware for three days that the plane was missing, thought it imperative to maintain absolute secrecy concerning the valuable U-2 program. The irony of this, says Ambrose, "was that the U-2 was no secret to the Soviets, and had not been since the very first flight, back in 1956." Believing that the craft's pilot, Gary Francis Powers, could not possibly still be alive to refute his story, the president decided to try a cover-up. He had NASA issue a statement claiming that the lost U-2 was a high-flying weather research craft that had erroneously strayed into Soviet airspace. When Soviet Premier Khrushchev countered with photographs of the downed plane and evidence that pilot Powers was still alive, Eisenhower was caught publicly in his lie.

One result of the U-2 incident was revitalization of Democratic attacks on administration foreign policy, and its secrecy in conducting that policy. Under the chairmanship of Fulbright, the Senate Foreign Relations Committee launched yet another full-dress investigation. Testimony in the hearings was not made public, and the report, while critical of the administration's response to the shootdown, did no serious damage to Eisenhower's control over the CIA. But the episode gave the Democrats a splendid opportunity to dissect administration policies, and to portray Eisenhower as not in full control of government policies and actions abroad.

The U-2 incident torpedoed the summit meeting scheduled for Paris in mid-May of 1960. In early 1958, Eisenhower had tentatively agreed to a second summit and, in an effort to stimulate progress toward a nuclear testing limitation agreement with the Soviets, followed up by instituting a unilateral moratorium on further American testing that lasted until the end of his presidency. Then, in 1959, he had acceded to Khrushchev's oft-stated hope to visit the United States. The Soviet leader's resulting ten-day visit in September 1959 was the occasion for true media hype, providing a forum for Khrushchev to strut and posture daily before the assembled world press, but producing little in the way of progress toward substantive Soviet-American agreement except that a four-power summit would be held in Paris in May 1960. The cancellation of that summit in the wake of the U-2 incident represented a major setback to gradually developing hopes for a lasting test-ban agreement and settlement of the vexing German question.

On another Cold War front, Eisenhower averted serious Democratic attacks by acting with a resoluteness matching all but the most strident red baiters in the Congress. Fidel Castro, whose revolutionary movement against Cuba's American-backed dictator, Fulgencio Batista, succeeded in January 1959, at first confronted the administration with a puzzling problem: whether to recognize the new regime or delay reaction, hoping a more obviously pro-American figure might topple Castro. After deciding for pragmatic reasons to extend diplomatic recognition, the president maintained a hopeful attitude toward Castro through the spring of 1959, despite the growing anti-Americanism of the Cuban leader's speeches. By summer, Eisenhower had decided not to recommend extension of the Sugar Act, which had guaranteed to Cuban producers over 70 percent of the American market. Meanwhile, Vice President Nixon—whose anti-Communist zeal where Latin America was concerned had been strengthened by the assaults his entourage had suffered at the hands of leftist anti-American protesters during visits to Peru and Venezuela in 1958—took leadership of a "get tough" faction within the administration. By March of 1960, their position bolstered by the strengthening economic bonds between Havana and Moscow, the hardliners prevailed. Eisenhower, in a counterpoint to his idealistic quest for a test-ban treaty with the Soviets, resolved to undermine the Castro regime in Cuba.

To carry out this policy, the president requested authority from Congress to reduce Cuba's sugar quota, and, though it was not known at the time, unleashed the CIA against Castro. The latter decision led directly to the calamitously unsuccessful invasion by Cuban counterrevolutionaries at the Bay of Pigs in April 1961, a disaster for which Eisenhower's White House successor took most of the blame. Another facet of the strategy, not disclosed till the 1970s, was a series of bungled attempts to assassinate Castro. These top-secret CIA operations against Castro's regime underscored the futility of congressional efforts to bring "Ike's spies" under control in the aftermath of the U-2 incident. Meanwhile, the authorization to reduce the Cuban sugar quota was approved with bipartisan support in July 1960.

As Robert Divine has observed, the Cuban challenge marked the onset of a time when Eisenhower "found himself the prisoner of [world] events." The tensions with Castro would lead, by January 1961, to a break in Cuban-American diplomatic relations, while a successful rebellion in the Congo and rapidly growing Communist strength in Indochina confronted the outgoing administration with insoluble dilemmas on two other continents. After the spring of 1960, writes Divine, Eisenhower "was unable to regain the momentum he had been trying to create toward easing Cold War tensions." And, despite his nearly incredible continuing popularity with the voters, he was incapable of controlling the flow of political events that led inexorably to his greatest frustration of all: GOP defeat in the election of 1960 and the restoration of the Fair Deal in different packaging.

President versus Congress

From early 1959 on, domestic issues were ensnarled in the politics of the 1960 presidential contest. The Twenty-second Amendment, which made Eisenhower the first president to be barred from running again, removed any doubt that the White House was up for grabs. Moreover, even though presidential contenders of the past had frequently come from the ranks of the nation's governors, virtually all of the leading possibilities for 1960 were already in Washington. Their presence in the arena of daily government ensured that campaign considerations colored every policy debate.

The Senate in particular was a snakepit. On the Democratic side, Majority Leader Johnson was a candidate of undisguised and unending ambition, no matter how fervently he disclaimed it. Kennedy, Humphrey, Symington, and one or

two others with less reason for optimism also harbored White
House hopes. The Republicans had different problems, since
Vice President Richard Nixon was considered by most to be
a shoo-in for his party's top spot in 1960, despite an expected
challenge by New York Governor Nelson Rockefeller. For in
the Senate was Barry Goldwater of Arizona, the darling of the
party's right wing (which had plans of its own for the years
beyond 1960). Reelected by an impressive margin in 1958
despite the Democratic sweep, Goldwater served as a natural
rallying point for revived GOP obstructionism in the Eighty-
sixth Congress.

Two additional political complications loomed. Eisenhower, deeply distressed at the outcome of the 1958 elections,
had publicly promised a crusade—alone, if necessary—to keep
federal spending down. Secondly, the North-South split in the
Democratic party seemed likely to grow wider yet, as a new
militant mood emerged in the black community and the continued postponement of civil rights questions appeared impossible. The outlook for harmony in 1959 and 1960 was, to
say the least, poor.

With the recession of 1957–1958 giving way to recovery
by January 1959, Eisenhower did not even mention unemployment in his State of the Union address. Instead, he emphasized fiscal orthodoxy, a concept he soon fleshed out by
presenting a bare-bones $77 billion budget for fiscal 1960. Ad-
ministration revenue estimates projected a very slight budget
surplus. The president's proposals, and especially his bulldog-
like efforts to block spending increases, produced a Democratic
counteroffensive to foster economic growth. "[A] reasonable
and sane public policy aimed at . . . vigorous expansion of the
economy," declared the majority on the Joint Economic Committee in March 1959, "should not be unduly deterred by the
possibility of future inflation." Ultimately, the president was
forced to accept a budget for fiscal 1960 of just over $79 billion;
through firm resolve and generous use of his vetoes, he achieved
a surplus anyway. Casualties to presidential veto in 1959 included two public works bills, two housing measures, and a

farm bill. Other important measures suffered a like fate in 1960, though in that year the exigencies of party politics led Eisenhower to relent and approve, against his better judgment, a $500,000 increase in defense.spending.

The congressional majority also notched some victories over the White House. In 1959, Eisenhower was badly shaken by the rejection of his nomination of Lewis Strauss for appointment as secretary of commerce. Strauss, a controversial member of the Atomic Energy Commission earlier in Eisenhower's presidency, had made many enemies with his arrogant, outspoken manner. One of the most persistent (and dangerous), as it turned out, was Senator Clinton Anderson (New Mexico), who quarterbacked the 49–46 vote denying confirmation. Strauss was the first cabinet nominee since 1925 to be turned down. Near the end of the 1959 session, Congress also overrode an Eisenhower veto for the first time, pushing through a water resources projects bill by votes of 72–23 in the Senate and 280–121 in the House. Democrats banded together overwhelmingly in both houses, and were joined by enough western and plains Republicans to overturn the veto.

Despite these struggles, there were still occasional instances when president and Congress could come to constructive agreement. Two examples were statehood bills for Alaska and Hawaii, approved in 1958 and 1959, respectively. Though little remarked at the time, these measures were a major achievement of the Eisenhower years.

Jockeying for position in the 1960 presidential race dramatically affected legislative activity in the area of labor-management relations. The Landrum-Griffin Act of 1959, the first revision of labor law since Taft-Hartley, was an administration victory brought about at least in part by a desire on the part of Republicans and some leading Democrats to embarrass John F. Kennedy, who was sponsoring a more prounion measure. By 1958, Kennedy was already running hard for his party's 1960 nomination. Having been a highly visible member of the McClellan Committee (a select Senate panel established in 1957 to investigate union racketeering), he hoped to secure labor support through passage of a bill that would safeguard union finances from abuse. At the urging of labor leaders, Kennedy had included a number of "sweeteners"—for example, a provision ensuring workers the right to a secret ballot on whether to have union representation at all. In 1958, after addition of an anti-Communist rider, the bill swept through the Senate, 88–1. But the conservative coalition in the House blocked further action. The next year, McClellan, a conservative southerner whose "expert" credentials on labor had been established by his chairing of the select committee, succeeded in adding a number of unfriendly provisions to the Kennedy bill. In no mood to help JFK build his reputation, Johnson silently assisted the conservative forces. The House then substituted its own, more strongly antiunion measure, the Landrum-Griffin bill, most of which became law in September 1959.

The Landrum-Griffin Act, no longer bearing Kennedy's name (nor much of his imprint), was considered a disastrous bill by organized labor. It did, in fact, strengthen prohibitions on secondary boycotts and certain other kinds of activities by which stronger unions might assist weaker ones; it also increased the power of state authorities (frequently less friendly to labor than the federal government) to adjudicate jurisdictional disputes between unions. Its antiracketeering provisions, however, were not necessarily inimical to the interests of workers and honest labor leaders, nor were the controls placed on labor-management collusion. Undeniably, by the late 1950s, both government officials and the general public were less friendly to labor interests than had been true in the preceding two decades. The slow rate of growth in union membership after World War II (from 14 million to less than 17 million) in those years reflected the hostile environment. The real problems for labor, however, were more structural than political; unemployment due to automation, a decline in the relative number of blue-collar workers in the labor force, and the fact that the most readily organizable blocs of workers had long since been unionized. Given such problems, the Landrum-Griffin Act was hardly as critical a problem for unions as they labeled it at the time.

The issue of civil rights also became entangled in the maneuvering of aspirants for the presidency. By early 1960, a climate for change had been established. The back of massive resistance was broken, and black-led protest was growing rapidly. The sit-in movement, begun by a small group of black college students in Greensboro, North Carolina, on February 1, 1960, spread rapidly throughout the South, leading to violence in some cities. A new organization born of the sit-ins, the Student Non-violent Coordinating Committee (SNCC), represented a significant new social and political force. As Robert Burk has recounted, Eisenhower was noncommittal on SNCC and the sit-in phenomenon. Acknowledging the legitimacy of the protesters' general goals, he insisted that the federal government should address itself only to ending discrimination in spheres of "public charter."

With the president reluctant to take leadership, hopes for meaningful civil rights legislation rested with the Democrats. The ambitions of Lyndon Johnson again helped ensure action. A southerner who needed a broader constituency to win the White House, Johnson took a new interest in civil rights in the Eighty-sixth Congress. Though his own 1959 proposal for a federal Community Relations Service (to serve as a "reconciliation" force in areas suffering civil rights disturbances) got nowhere, he lent an important hand to passage of a limited administration-backed voting rights bill in early 1960. With the help of Minority Leader Everett Dirksen, the Democratic leadership kept the bill limited in scope and secured its easy passage, overcoming opposition from both southerners and disappointed northern liberals. The 1960 Civil Rights Act became law in May. "[B]y any standard," concluded *Congressional Quarterly,* the bill was only "a modest modification" of the 1957 law, providing for court protection of voting rights but little else.

End of an Era: The Election of 1960

Presidential nominating politics consumed the attention of the nation's elected leaders in 1960. The contest on the Democratic side promised to be especially interesting and spirited. Two rivals squared off against each other in the primaries: liberal favorite Hubert Humphrey, who declared his candidacy at the end of December 1959, and Kennedy, who—after two years of assiduous stumping for delegates—officially entered the fray just days after Humphrey. Symington and Johnson, whose aspirations were widely known, avoided the primaries and declared in March and July, respectively. Waiting in the wings was the nostalgic favorite, Stevenson.

Kennedy, the choice of many southerners for the vice presidential nomination in 1956, had been hard at work to project a more liberal image but was free of any ideological label. In *The Democrats,* Parmet describes the Massachusetts senator as "a virtual stereotype of the nonideological man who had come into vogue during the 1950s and stressed power and its implementation rather than ideas." Kennedy held a decided advantage in financial resources, particularly those of his wealthy father, Joseph P. Kennedy, and in organization.

Kennedy's first two decisive primary victories over Humphrey, in New Hampshire and Wisconsin, were treated as suspect by the media because he had the advantages of being a regional favorite son in the former, and of being a Catholic candidate in a heavily Catholic electorate in the latter. In West Virginia, however, he enjoyed neither of these special assets. His routing of Humphrey in that state's May 10 primary ended the two-man race. On the day after his defeat, the crestfallen Humphrey dropped out, hurling allegations of vote buying at the Kennedy organizers which, though believable enough, were never substantiated.

No other Democrat could mount a real threat to JFK as his juggernaut rolled on toward the July 11 convention in Los Angeles. Johnson, adhering to his initial strategy, waited till the last minute to announce, in the hope of bringing together a winning coalition of southerners and others opposed to a Kennedy candidacy. But he was too late, with too little. A boomlet for the publicly reluctant but privately very willing Stevenson, punctuated by a wild floor demonstration at the convention, was stillborn, and the junior senator from Massachusetts was nominated on the first ballot. Observers—including pros in both parties—were then stunned when LBJ, who had said he would never accept second place on the Democratic ticket, did just that. One prominent spectator was distinctly unimpressed with the Democratic pairing. LBJ, remarked Eisenhower to a friend, "is a small man. . . . superficial and opportunistic"; and Eisenhower would "do almost anything to avoid turning my chair and the country over to Kennedy."

The platform adopted by the Democrats reflected the preferences of party liberals, calling for increased federal action to bring about economic growth, higher spending levels for defense, and efforts to end discrimination based on race, creed, or color. The civil rights plank, in fact, was the most liberal in the party's history. Closing the convention with a well-crafted acceptance speech, Kennedy embraced the ambitious platform and called for a positive approach to "the New Frontier" that was here, "whether we seek it or not."

Within the Republican party, Nixon's nomination was inevitable. Having labored long and tirelessly on behalf of the party, he was about to reap his reward from a loyal organization. As Eisenhower's several biographers agree, the president himself still regarded Nixon with ambivalence, though in the end he preferred him to all viable alternatives. "[T]here was always a 'but' in the Eisenhower-Nixon relationship," says Ambrose. Since the president could not induce his first choice, Robert Anderson, to become a candidate, that seemed to leave only Nelson Rockefeller, whose "free-spending" instincts and criticisms of administration defense policies were anathema to Eisenhower.

Rockefeller, fresh from a half-million-plurality victory in the 1958 New York gubernatorial election, lusted for his party's presidential nomination and had gone after it with a vengeance in 1959. Disappointed by the lack of response from party chieftains, he withdrew from the race late that year. He was intent, however, that Nixon and the party pay obeisance to his policy views, especially in the areas of defense, civil rights, and economic growth—in all of which he took a more activist stance than the vice president. Using the implied threat of reentering the contest and disrupting party unity, he coerced Nixon into meeting with him just prior to the convention, scheduled to convene in Chicago on July 25. From the conclave came a series of platform statements endorsed by the two party leaders. "If you don't think that [document] represents my views," boasted Rockefeller upon arriving at Chicago, "you're crazy." Conservatives agreed with the governor. Goldwater styled the agreement "the Munich of the Republican party," while the Chicago *Tribune* trumpeted "Grant Surrenders to Lee."

The GOP platform committee dutifully included most of the statements agreed upon by Nixon and Rockefeller. The defense plank, for example—to the intense irritation of the president—included the phrase, "there is no price ceiling on America's security." And on civil rights, the 1960 plank was considerably more liberal than the party position of four years earlier, even though, as Burk writes, "Nixon's actual philosophy of the role of the federal government in civil rights differed but marginally from Eisenhower's."

Nixon was nominated unanimously on the first ballot, but not before party conservatives enjoyed a long moment in the limelight. Goldwater, whose postelection analysis after the GOP disaster in 1958 was that the party should "quit copying the New Deal," had produced a book in 1960 (*The Conscience of a Conservative*) that immediately gained acceptance as the right wing's manifesto. Placed in nomination at the convention (and assured of at least 300 votes), the Arizonan withdrew, but he delivered a blockbuster speech pregnant with significance for the party's future. The party platform was imperfect, he conceded, but far superior to the Democrats' "blueprint for socialism." He urged his fellow conservatives to give Nixon full support in the 1960 election, but advised in closing: "Let's get to work if we want to take this party back—and I think we can." The vice president, once nominated, selected as his running mate United Nations Ambassador Henry Cabot Lodge, who had been a prime mover in the 1952 Eisenhower movement.

The 1960 campaign revolved around four issues: the adequacy of American defense, aggressiveness in U.S. foreign policy, the dilemma of civil rights, and the need for economic growth. On all four, Kennedy—as challenger—took the initiative, and Nixon was left to defend the policies of the Eisenhower administration. This made him appear, perhaps unfairly, the candidate of the status quo. In the area of national defense, for example, Kennedy kept up the drumfire about a "missile gap" that had helped him secure the nomination. Eisenhower deeply resented this impugning of his defense policies, and it was probably the Democratic candidate's frequent charges of a "gap" that accounted for the retiring president's unforgiving attitude towards him. Nixon, despite his earlier close identification with the anti-Communist right and his more recent effort to pacify Rockefeller by calling for additional defense dollars, was just too closely associated with the administration record to take the offensive on the issue. His stance seemed ambiguous, as he criticized the Democrats for "selling America short," while implying that he would increase defense spending.

The same relative positioning of the candidates prevailed on foreign policy issues, with Kennedy taking a "hard line" approach on the questions of how to handle Khrushchev and Castro. On China, the Democrats took a somewhat different tack, criticizing the administration for dashing too eagerly to the defense of Quemoy and Matsu and implying that "better communication" was needed with the People's Republic. Nixon, again, presented the best rationales he could for administration policies, all the while imploring Eisenhower to effect a bold stroke against Castro, to resolve not only the

Cuban problem but perhaps a major campaign difficulty as well. In fact, on both defense and foreign policy issues, there seemed little to choose between the candidates. Both actively accepted the challenge of winning the Cold War, as they tried to outdo each other in both militance and resolve. More than any before or since, 1960 was the quintessential Cold War campaign.

The key domestic issues were the state of the economy and civil rights. Nixon, again with his back to the wall, argued for the soundness of Eisenhower's conservative fiscal policies, while Kennedy, with obvious relish, repeatedly issued a call to "get this country moving again." A mild economic downturn in the middle of the campaign gave the Democrat's theme particular urgency. Civil rights also presented the challenger with opportunities to condemn the administration for inaction, but the Democrats, too, were vulnerable, since their southern wing was unwaveringly hostile to legislation beneficial to blacks and other minorities. Kennedy shared, to a lesser degree, Nixon's wariness about alienating southern whites by taking too unequivocal a stand on civil rights, as his choice of Johnson as running mate revealed.

When the postconvention final session of the Eighty-sixth Congress failed to produce any legislative action on civil rights, Kennedy was unruffled, explaining on September 1 that the Democratic majority had "not tried to match the eleventh hour Republican tactic of substituting staged political maneuvering for effective legislation." Observing that "no significant civil rights measure could have been passed," he added: "We believe our credentials are clear." To counter a possibly too-cautious image, on the other hand, Kennedy sniped at Eisenhower for not ending discrimination in housing with "a stroke of his pen," and, late in the campaign, made a dramatic sympathy phone call to Coretta Scott King while her husband was imprisoned in Georgia on a trumped-up charge. A more pointed follow-up call from his brother Robert to the judge who had jailed King secured King's release, and served as highly effective propaganda for the Democrats with black voters in the closing days of the campaign. Meanwhile, Nixon—after successfully pressing at the Republican convention for a strong civil rights plank—hedged on the issue during the campaign.

Kennedy's Catholicism surfaced as a significant issue in the campaign. When a group of conservative Protestant ministers issued a statement of "concern" about the papal influences that might follow the election of a Roman Catholic, the senator countered with a gutsy rebuttal of the "religious issue" before the Greater Ministerial Association in Houston, Texas. Addressing that skeptical group on September 12, Kennedy repeated his frequent assertion that he believed in absolute separation of church and state, and promised to oppose the granting of federal aid to parochial schools. The Houston performance failed to neutralize the religious issue, but public airing of the matter had a healthy effect on the tone of the campaign.

In 1960, television played a much greater role than it had in the Eisenhower elections. The innovation of four televised candidates' debates contributed to Nixon's defeat, even though observers at the time and those who later studied their content and impact agree that neither candidate "won" them. Watched by audiences of between 61 and 70 million, the debates reinforced the "image" of each of the two candidates. Kennedy's coolness and Ivy-toned good looks accomplished more than six months of Madison Avenue commercials could have. By contrast, Nixon's ill-concealed five-o'clock shadow, nervous expression, and perspiring upper lip did him in. Collectively, the debates between the two established the Democratic challenger, in Parmet's phrase, as "a rookie with championship promise." At least as important as their influence on individual voter decisions was the fact that the debates stimulated tremendous interest in the election. Statistics showed that voters newly entering the electorate in 1960 tended to support Kennedy in disproportionate numbers.

The 1960 election produced an extremely narrow margin of victory for Kennedy, who won by just under 115,000 votes out of the nearly 69 million cast (49.72 percent to Nixon's

49.55 percent). The electoral vote was less close (303–219). In congressional races, the Democrats did well, though they were unable to repeat their sweep of 1958. They held on to large majorities in both houses: 263–174 in the House (a loss of twenty seats, largely as a result of the GOP's recovering its "normal" seats lost in the swamping two years earlier), and 64–36 in the Senate (a loss of two seats, in Delaware and Wyoming). Incumbents in both parties fared exceptionally well.

Much was made of the limited role Eisenhower had played in the campaign, the common assumption being that had he helped Nixon more—had he *wanted* to help more—he could have made the difference. This observation is questionable on two counts. It was wrong to assume that Eisenhower was unwilling to help. He and Nixon had agreed early that Eisenhower would assist, as he ultimately did, with several speeches in large cities in the final stages of the campaign, capping his efforts with a televised speech on Nixon's behalf. More important, however, it is doubtful that Ike's greater presence in the campaign, popular as he was, could have helped the vice president. Such a role for Eisenhower would only have underscored, visibly and repeatedly, that Nixon was Nixon, not a surrogate Eisenhower. Moreover, as Ambrose has perceptively noted, Eisenhower's propensity to dwell on the past, and to defend his own achievements, would not have answered the needs of Nixon, facing so aggressive a challenger as JFK.

A study by Philip Converse and his colleagues at the Survey Research Center (SRC) provides a sound analysis of the 1960 outcome. Among the most significant "surface characteristics" of the election, they note, were the very high turnout, most especially in the South, and "stronger Republican voting at the presidential level." The single cause accounting for these factors, the SRC analysts demonstrate, was religion. Kennedy's Catholicism won him extra votes in the North, but cost him massively in the South, while the force of the issue helped to mobilize voters in unprecedented numbers, again particularly in Dixie. The study concluded that this election, which "reinstated" the normal Democratic majority, nonetheless failed to produce the "expected" vote for that majority. Overall, the authors demonstrate, Kennedy lost just over 2 percent of the vote nationally due to his religion. But the election may have hinged on the fact that Kennedy gained thousands of *pro*-Catholic votes in the big cities in the northern industrial states, including several he carried narrowly, such as Michigan, New Jersey, New York, Pennsylvania, and Illinois. In Illinois, however, "creative" vote tabulating by Chicago's Democratic mayor, Richard Daley, may have been of even more assistance.

In an election as close as the Kennedy-Nixon race, any single factor that produced a vote shift can be seen as decisive. Even with sophisticated tools of analysis, so complex and overlapping are voters' motives that no definitive answer emerges. For instance, in addition to religion, the impact of race and racial issues on the 1960 election has been much discussed. The black vote, which returned heavily to the Democrats in 1960 after a slight fall-off to Eisenhower four years earlier, undoubtedly contributed significantly to Kennedy's victories in the important urban states. In the South, however, which gave JFK eighty-one crucially important electoral votes, it is unclear whether white or black ballots made the difference. Many have credited Lyndon Johnson for carrying the white South for the Democratic ticket. As seasoned a political observer as Richard Russell predicted as much on the eve of the election. On the other hand, it can be argued that the South's 1.4 million black voters were decisive. Black ballots may well have made the difference for Kennedy, for example, in South Carolina and Texas. A final answer is not readily apparent on this point, but what can be said is that in 1960 there occurred neither white rebellion in the "black belt" nor huge gains for the Democrats among black voters. The Democrats' balancing act on civil rights worked.

What did it all signify? The Democrats were divided: liberals felt it was a new beginning, while southern conservatives were wary but took comfort in Lyndon Johnson's presence in the administration. Republicans, especially the party's right wing, were bitterly disappointed. "We cannot win as a dime-store copy of the opposition's platform," said Barry Goldwater. "We must be different." Concerning the future of Richard Nixon, William Miller, chairman of the Republican Congressional Campaign Committee, demonstrated twenty-twenty foresight: "Any man who, at 47, comes within 300,000 [sic] votes of winning the presidency—for a party that is greatly outnumbered—has to be reckoned with. It's far too early to bury Dick Nixon."

It was also too early to bury Eisenhower. The president retained enormous personal popularity to the end. A Gallup poll taken a fortnight before the election gave him a public approval rating of nearly 60 percent, and of 90 percent among Republicans. TRB, the *New Republic's* resident liberal pundit, offered an unflattering explanation. Eisenhower's "popularity was undiminished," he wrote, "for he could honestly say that he had not squandered it on any difficult or unpopular cause. And no president in history had left more unsolved problems for his successor." The president's Commission on National Goals, appointed in February 1960 to produce a "broad outline of national objectives and programs for the next decade," implied in its report a few weeks after the election that much remained to be done. Still, TRB's verdict was too harsh. Eisenhower had inherited problems from Truman (the Korean War, for example), as Truman had from FDR (the emerging Cold War). Such things are very difficult to quantify or compare.

Eisenhower's disappointment with the verdict of the voters was tempered by his eagerness to escape the burdens of the presidency and retire to Gettysburg. He never became an admirer of John F. Kennedy, but he relented somewhat in his judgment once the voters had spoken. Two days after the election, according to Eisenhower's longtime secretary, Ann Whitman, the president confided to his brother Milton that "at first he had felt that the work of eight years was down the drain." But, he added, Kennedy seemed to be "talking more responsibly since the election than he did before." Never one to retreat unnecessarily, the president told his brother he was "going to put in a balanced budget—and see what the new Administration [would do] to that."

The election results of 1960 perfectly captured the moment. Having won with a scant 49.72 percent, Kennedy had neither a mandate nor a majority. Indeed, no clear majority had existed in American politics since FDR's death. In that sense, the politics of the years between 1945 and 1960 comprised a seamless fabric. Truman, like Kennedy, had been elected by fewer than half the voters, and had been hobbled by opposition Congresses—sometimes in name, always in fact. Eisenhower had registered two victories of landslide proportions, but as virtually all commentators observed, these were personal triumphs. The voters who overwhelmingly elected Eisenhower ensured that his views would be countered by a legislative branch of opposite inclinations. Both Truman and Eisenhower led with strength, but in the end they could not move the nation very far because the nation did not wish to move. Victory in a world war and the prospect of boundless economic growth had seemed to render change unnecessary.

Now the nation was stirring. It began by electing a dynamic young president on little basis other than his exciting if vague promises to do the things that had been too long left undone. John F. Kennedy, noted a news magazine, had been "given a blank check drawn on a sound and thriving nation." If even he moved cautiously in addressing the nation's accumulated problems, it was nonetheless clear that a new era was beginning. The years of balance, equilibrium, or stagnation—depending on one's perspective—were at an end. The sixties would be different, if not necessarily better.

CONCLUSION:

Reflections on a Political Era

"[T]he torch has been passed to a new generation of Americans," forty-three-year-old John F. Kennedy pronounced in his inaugural address. True enough. Kennedy and his immediate successors were born in the twentieth century and came to full maturity after the Great Depression. Their vision of America was, if not blindly optimistic, at least unbounded. The United States was a superpower, a leader among nations, and its economic progress was a given. Energy and confidence were hallmarks of the new political generation, and the people shared those traits. "In retrospect," Wilson Carey McWilliams wrote in a 1983 *American Quarterly* article, "America in the 1960s seems so *autonomous. . . .* sometimes it felt as if we could say damn-all to the world."

Truman and Eisenhower represented the last of an older ruling generation. Differing on many political issues, they were alike in important essentials. Both had been seasoned by the calamities of the Depression and World War II, and both realized the fragility of national strength. They suspected it was possible for a country—even a superpower—to overreach itself. Eisenhower's warning against the excesses of a growing military-industrial complex in his moving farewell address in 1961 reflected this sensitivity. On the other hand, as the first American leaders to have responsibility for nuclear weapons, both Truman and Eisenhower knew that, in at least one respect, the nation's ultimate power was irrefutable. These shared realizations exercised a common influence in their administrations, and shaped the political environment in which they led.

Neither one was a great president, if ratings must be given, but each had a strong impact on his times. Certain of their actions had a lasting impact: Truman's decisions to drop the atomic bomb, to develop the hydrogen bomb, to confront the problem of civil rights, and to expand the range of concerns addressed by the New Deal; Eisenhower's institutionalization of the national security apparatus, his decision to send troops into Little Rock, and his acceptance, on behalf of the GOP, of the general outlines of the modern welfare state. Though often stalemated by political opponents, both were strong, decisive leaders. Each held in check the forces of division in his party, and in the nation.

Historiographical trends have produced converging views of the two presidents. After undergoing a furious debunking by the New Left historians of the early 1970s, Truman's reputation has been restored to respectability and more. Eisenhower, whose standing with scholars was not very good when he left office, never suffered a debunking, and has enjoyed favorable treatment from recent historians, who agree that he was a skillful leader, even if they disagree with his politics. Only in the area of civil rights has Eisenhower received consistently low marks. In partial mitigation of his inaction in the cause of black rights, however, one historian who is critical, Alton Lee, concludes that, "in fairness . . . , it should be noted that Congress, the people's representatives, did even less than he to achieve integration." Throughout the Truman-Eisenhower years, the legislative branch maintained its own "deliberate speed" on the issue of civil rights.

The presidency itself was expanded and institutionalized to an unprecedented degree in the Truman and Eisenhower years. As Arthur Schlesinger has described in *The Imperial Presidency,* each of the two presidents reacted to foreign crises with broad assertions of executive power that swept aside congressional objections. Moreover, Truman was responsible for bringing order and permanence to the seemingly haphazard growth of the White House office during the New Deal years. He appointed a commission, headed by Herbert Hoover, to examine the need for governmental reorganization and, in 1949, successfully proposed legislation embodying that commission's recommendations. The resulting legislation made it a simple matter to reorganize the executive branch without significant congressional input. Institution of the NSC and CIA in the Truman years also further institutionalized (and insulated) the executive. Eisenhower continued to build in these directions by substantially increasing the White House staff, establishing a formal White House liaison with Congress, and successfully resisting investigative intrusions by invoking "executive privilege." Perhaps his most important contribution in this regard, however, was the innovative "area resolution," a device that effectively preempted congressional opposition to later executive actions. Indeed, the remarkable rise of the office of the presidency during the fifteen years following World War II was one of the major political achievements of the period.

Both Truman and Eisenhower also had significant impact on their parties. Alonzo Hamby has accurately observed that Truman "defended and advanced the objectives of American progressivism," in the face of "a postwar public apathetic toward new reform breakthroughs." The priorities of his presidency ensured that the national Democratic party would remain in the New Deal orbit, which in turn left the party well-positioned to respond to activist liberal leadership in the White House in the 1960s. Too, black Americans could for the first time believe that one of the major parties genuinely cared about their plight.

Similarly, Eisenhower's reluctant acceptance of much of the welfare state legitimized it in American politics, but his legacy to the party was somewhat different. As he spoke in general, commonsense terms about "modern Republicanism," vagueness was the key to his political success. The rigid opposition to even limited federal activity of the Old Guard Republicans could not have provided the basis for a viable political party in the postwar years; the social welfarism spawned by the New Deal had simply become too institutionalized. Through his ill-defined "modern Republicanism," Eisenhower made GOP hostility to big government both acceptable and respectable. He continually stressed his conservatism, and was never afraid to use the word. By the phrase "modern Republicanism," he explained to GOP National Chairman Meade Alcorn, he meant "only, of course, Republicanism adapted to the problems of today." At the end of the fifties, despite myths of a bipartisan consensus and the "end of ideology," the two major parties retained the basic differences that had characterized them since the days of the New Deal.

Both postwar presidents exercised strong leadership of American foreign policy, in substance and process. Numerous historians have noted similarities in the outcomes, if not the theory, of their Cold War policies. Truman and Acheson spoke of "containment," while Eisenhower and Dulles used the rhetoric of "liberation" and "massive retaliation," but the operational differences were sometimes slight. The Truman administration, like its successor, was willing to rely on "big bang" weapons technology, if necessary. Why else go ahead, as Truman did, with development of the H-bomb in 1950? Truman's reliance on conventional forces in Korea seemed to contrast with the "massive retaliation" posture with which Eisenhower is identified, but it should be remembered that Eisenhower only talked about employing nuclear weapons— he never used them. It was the marines, not nuclear warheads, that were deployed in Lebanon.

Both Truman and Eisenhower also spoke a great deal about

bipartisanship, and pointed to broad areas of agreement between themselves and the political opposition. But politics did
not "stop at the water's edge" during their presidencies. Just
as congressional Republicans distanced themselves from Truman on China policy and the uses of foreign aid, congressional
Democrats developed alternatives to Eisenhower's foreign policies. Specifically, they urged a greater sense of engagement in
the struggles of emerging nations, an emphasis on flexible response capability, and rejection of rigid, preannounced treaty
commitments. These Democratic themes would emerge more
clearly in the 1960s, when the party controlled both White
House and Congress.

The decade and a half following World War II was, in
many ways, the last hurrah for "politics as usual" in the United
States. Both voters and party organizations continued to behave in the postwar years much as they had during the decades
preceding World War II. Studies of the electorate of the fifties
by the Survey Research Center revealed only a moderate level
of political involvement by the voters, but widespread identification with one party or the other, and a strong tendency
to straight-ticket voting (except for president). These tenden-
cies would all be sharply changed after 1960.

If identification with a political party was still fashionable
during the Truman and Eisenhower years, however, ideological and class conflict were not. Ladd and Hadley, in *Transformations of the American Party System,* emphasize the "decline of class differences over salient policy questions" in the
1940s and 1950s. During the period, blacks shifted overwhelmingly into the Democratic party and southern whites showed
signs of breaking away in the opposite direction, but in overall
terms, the 1940s and 1950s were decades of political consol-
idation—a time, Ladd and Hadley observe, "when changes
initiated in the Depression and New Deal epoch were incor-
porated into a new political landscape." In turn, the new importance of black voters and the lesser connection between
class and partisan behavior helped to accelerate the coming of

a quite different, and less predictable, political dynamic in the sixties and thereafter.

The findings of a 1960 study, *The American Voter,* confirm the view that the years presided over by Truman and Eisenhower represented the end of an era. On the basis of an extensive analysis of political behavior during these years, the authors conclude that "the stabilities . . . were more important than the aspects of change." More than two decades—a generation, in American political life—would pass before that could be said again.

BIBLIOGRAPHICAL ESSAY

There exists no scholarly study that treats American political life in the years 1945–1960 as a single era. Good coverage is given to the period, however, by three narrative works on political history since 1945: William Leuchtenburg, *In the Shadow of FDR: From Harry Truman to Ronald Reagan* (1983); Herbert Parmet, *The Democrats: The Years After FDR* (1976); and David Reinhard, *The Republican Right Since 1945* (1983). Arthur M. Schlesinger's *The Imperial Presidency* (1973) also includes valuable coverage of the Truman and Eisenhower years, while Alonzo Hamby, *Liberalism and Its Challengers: FDR to Reagan* (1985) includes interesting biographical essays on key figures of the period.

On the other hand, both the Truman and Eisenhower presidencies have been written about extensively. The production of such works, in fact, has been increasing steadily, both stimulating and reflecting the rise of the two presidents' historical reputations.

The earliest authoritative work on the Truman administration was journalist Cabell Phillips's *The Truman Presidency: The History of a Triumphant Succession* (1966). Though an admiring work, Phillips's book is thorough and balanced in coverage, and has held up well. In 1973, however, it was partially superseded by Alonzo Hamby's *Beyond the New Deal: Harry S. Truman and American Liberalism.* Hamby made use of the rich resource materials at the Truman Library, and his study—while also favorable to Truman—is more analytical than Phillips's, especially in its attempt to place Truman within a political tradition. Other histories of the Truman years produced in the 1970s included Bert Cochran's *Harry Truman and the Crisis Presidency* (1973) and Athan Theoharis's *The Truman Presidency: The Origins of the Imperial Presidency and the National Security State* (1979), both somewhat selective, highly critical New Left treatments, and *Harry Truman* (1974), a predictably adoring—but nonetheless interesting— work by the president's daughter, Margaret Truman. A less ideological study, limited by its theme, is Richard Haynes, *The Awesome Power: Harry S. Truman as Commander in Chief* (1973).

In the late 1970s, Robert Donovan produced the first volume of an important two-part study of the Truman years. *Conflict and Crisis: The Presidency of Harry S. Truman, 1945– 1948* (1977) combines sound historical scholarship and excellent narrative style. In this volume and its equally meritorious sequel, *Tumultuous Years: The Presidency of Harry S. Truman, 1949–1953* (1982), Donovan provides a sympathetic yet realistic assessment of the thirty-third president. His study is the standard against which other works on the Truman presidency will be measured.

A recent solid, if briefer general treatment is Donald McCoy, *The Presidency of Harry S. Truman* (1984), one of the better entries in the University Press of Kansas series on presidential administrations. Other recent additions to Truman scholarship are Harold Gosnell, *Truman's Crises: A Political Biography of Harry S. Truman* (1980); Robert Underhill, *The Truman Persuasions* (1981); Robert H. Ferrell, *Harry S. Truman and the Modern American Presidency* (1983); and Roy Jenkins, *Truman* (1986).

The list of monographs on the Truman period has grown long. Valuable historiographical assessments of that literature, though now dated, are *The Truman Period as a Research Field* (1967), and a revised, updated edition, *The Truman Period as a Research Field: A Reappraisal, 1972* (1974), both edited by Richard Kirkendall and including essays by other leading scholars, some his former students. Substantial early monographs are Richard Davies, *Housing Reform During The Truman Administration* (1966); Allen Matusow, *Farm Policies and Politics in the Truman Years* (1967); Alton Lee, *Truman and Taft-Hartley: A Question of Mandate* (1966); Arthur McClure, *The Truman Administration and the Problems of Postwar Labor, 1945–1948* (1969); and Susan Hartmann, *Truman and the Eightieth Congress* (1971). A useful collection of essays is Francis Heller, ed., *Economics and the Truman Administration* (1981).

The 1948 election is a fascinating story that has often been told. Two interesting studies are Irwin Ross, *The Loneliest Campaign: The Truman Victory of 1948* (1968), and Allen Yarnell, *Democrats and Progressives: The 1948 Presidential Election as a Test of Postwar Liberalism* (1974). A narrower, but still useful study is Robert Divine, *Foreign Policy and U.S. Presidential Elections, 1940–1948* (1974). Also valuable on the 1948 election, and on the Truman-Wallace conflict generally, are Norman Markowitz, *The Rise and Fall of the People's Century: Henry A. Wallace and American Liberalism, 1941–1948* (1973); Richard Walton, *Henry Wallace, Harry Truman, and the Cold War* (1976); and J. Samuel Walker, *Henry A. Wallace and American Foreign Policy* (1976).

Monographic treatments of strongly contrasting viewpoints have appeared on the subjects of civil rights and anti-Communist activities in the Truman years. William Berman's *The Politics of Civil Rights in the Truman Administration* (1970) takes the president to task for making too limited a commitment to minorities. Donald McCoy and Richard Ruetten, however, in *Quest and Response: Minority Rights and the Truman Administration* (1973), argue that significant civil rights advances occurred in the Truman years. The impact of the civil rights issue on party politics is the subject of David Garson's *The Democratic Party and the Politics of Sectionalism, 1941–1948* (1974).

Truman's role in the anti-Communist drive of the late 1940s has been examined in two very critical studies: Athan Theoharis, *Seeds of Repression: Harry S. Truman and the Origins of McCarthyism* (1971), and Richard Freeland, *The Truman Doctrine and the Origins of McCarthyism: Foreign Policy, Domestic Politics, and Internal Security, 1946–1948* (1972). A more favorable assessment of Truman as a defender of civil liberties is Alan Harper, *The Politics of Loyalty: The White House and the Communist Issue, 1946–1952* (1969). Several works on McCarthyism, cited later, are also informative on the Truman administration's handling of the threat of subversion.

Four additional works on important domestic issues in the Truman era are Maeva Marcus, *Truman and the Steel Seizure Case: The Limits of Presidential Power* (1977); Monte Poen, *Harry S. Truman Versus the Medical Lobby: The Genesis of Medicare* (1979); Andrew Dunar, *The Truman Scandals and the Politics of Morality* (1984); and William Moore, *The Kefauver Committee and the Politics of Crime, 1950–1952* (1974).

The origins of the Cold War have been a subject of great interest to historians. A few general works deserve special mention for their excellence. *The United States and the Origins of the Cold War, 1941–1947* (1972), by John Gaddis, has deservedly become a standard for its reasoned, realistic discussion of the intersection of American public opinion with the political process and foreign policy formulation in those years. Another effective overview is Thomas Paterson, *On Every Front: The Making of the Cold War* (1979), which strikes a balance between the earlier uncritical interpretations and New Left critiques of American motives and policies.

A classic early New Left work is Gar Alperovitz, *Atomic Diplomacy: Hiroshima and Potsdam,* which harshly criticizes Truman's decision to unleash atomic bombs on Japan. Originally published in 1965, *Atomic Diplomacy* argues that possession of the bomb led the United States to behave in an overly aggressive fashion toward the Soviets, thereby beginning the Cold War. Among the most influential of the new, more balanced studies on the same subject are Martin Sherwin, *A World Destroyed: The Atomic Bomb and the Grand Alliance* (1977), which views Truman as pragmatic rather than scheming and focuses on the intertwining of scientific developments and the nation's diplomatic activities; and Gregg Herken, *The Winning Weapon: The Atomic Bomb in the Cold War, 1945–1950* (1980), an excellent study of the evolution of U.S. strategy and diplomacy with respect to nuclear weapons.

Another first-rate general study of U.S. policy making in the early Cold War is Daniel Yergin's *Shattered Peace: The Origins of the Cold War and the National Security State* (1978), a nonpolemical narrative which describes the institutionalization of Cold War precepts in American political life. Lloyd C. Gardner, *Architects of Illusion: Men and Ideas in American Foreign Policy, 1941–1949* (1970), is excellent on the ideological differences and accommodations that underlay Truman's policies toward the Soviets.

Two books of great value for understanding the broad political environment and evolving Cold War policies of the Truman (and Eisenhower) years are John Gaddis, *Strategies of Containment: A Critical Appraisal of Postwar American National Security Policy* (1982), and a collection of original essays edited by Norman Graebner, *The National Security: Its Theory and Practice, 1945–1960* (1986). Also useful is an earlier collection edited by Thomas Paterson, *Cold War Critics: Alternatives to American Foreign Policy in the Truman Years* (1971), which includes thoughtful essays on the thinking of Taft, Wallace, and several other figures outside the administrations.

United States policy towards Asia was an intensely political subject in the Truman years, and the subject has spawned some good books. Among these are William Stueck, *The Road to Confrontation: American Policy Toward China and Korea, 1947–1950* (1981), and Nancy Tucker, *Patterns in the Dust: Chinese-American Relations and the Recognition Controversy, 1949–1950* (1983).

A good recent study of the Korean War, including its

political aspects, is Burton Kaufman, *The Korean War: Challenges in Crisis, Credibility and Command* (1986). Also valuable is Francis Heller, ed., *The Korean War: A 25-Year Perspective* (1977). Ronald Caridi, *The Korean War and American Politics: The Republican Party as a Case Study* (1968), and Rosemary Foot, *The Wrong War: American Policy and the Dimensions of the Korean Conflict, 1950–1953* (1985) are more limited works. Robert Donovan pays attention to political ramifications in *Nemesis: Truman and Johnson in the Coils of War in Asia* (1984), but he is selective, attempting to draw parallels between the military escalations in Korea and Vietnam. John Spanier's *The Truman-MacArthur Controversy and the Korean War* (1959) has not been superseded by any later work on its subject.

The interplay of foreign policy issues and congressional partisan politics during the Truman years is the general subject of both Athan Theoharis, *The Yalta Myths: An Issue in U.S. Politics, 1945–1955* (1970), and Justus Doenecke, *Not to the Swift: The Old Isolationists in the Cold War Era* (1979). On the political considerations related to Truman's policy toward the new state of Israel, two books have appeared: John Snetsinger, *Truman, the Jewish Vote, and the Creation of Israel* (1974), and Zvi Ganin, *Truman, American Jewry, and Israel, 1945–1948* (1979).

The literature on the Eisenhower administration is becoming voluminous, though the first works by historians did not appear until the 1970s. The journalistic treatments, the best of which is Robert Donovan's anecdotal *Eisenhower: The Inside Story* (1965), were supplanted in 1972 by Herbert Parmet's revisionist *Eisenhower and the American Crusades.* (The term "revisionist," when applied to the literature on Eisenhower, refers not to a New Left critique of his foreign or domestic policies, but rather to an emphasis on his leadership skills as president and party leader.) Parmet's work was quickly followed by two other studies of Eisenhower's presidency. Peter Lyon's *Eisenhower: Portrait of the Hero* (1974) is harshly critical, portraying Eisenhower as an ineffective leader in the

White House, especially on domestic matters. On foreign policy, Lyon sees evidence of stronger leadership but criticizes Eisenhower for exacerbating the Cold War. Charles Alexander's 1975 book, *Holding the Line: The Eisenhower Era, 1952–1961* (1975), is much less critical, though still reflecting to a degree the earlier prevailing view that he was "above party" and not an especially energetic leader. Good on the Eisenhower-Nixon relationship is Garry Wills, *Nixon Agonistes* (1969).

Three full-scale scholarly treatments of the Eisenhower presidency have appeared since the late 1970s. Both Elmo Richardson, *The Presidency of Dwight D. Eisenhower* (1979), and Alton Lee, *Dwight D. Eisenhower: Soldier and Statesman* (1981), are concise accounts that accept some of the revisionist views of Ike. The third—and best—overall treatment is the second volume of Stephen Ambrose's biography, *Eisenhower: The President* (1984). Ambrose presents Ike as especially well informed and capable in foreign affairs, though somewhat less effective in domestic matters. A recent, selective study is Fred Greenstein's *The Hidden Hand Presidency: Eisenhower as Leader* (1982), which argues more strongly than even most revisionist studies that Eisenhower dominated his administration by using the technique of behind-the-scenes manipulation. An influential article on the thirty-fourth president's political views is Robert Griffith, "Dwight D. Eisenhower and the Corporate Commonwealth," *American Historical Review* 87 (1982): 87–122.

Most works that have examined McCarthy have concluded that his rise and fall both resulted from partisan and institutional forces greater than those exerted by the Eisenhower administration. Early studies presenting this theme were Michael Paul Rogin, *The Intellectuals and McCarthy: The Radical Specter* (1967); Robert Griffith, *The Politics of Fear: Joseph R. McCarthy and the Senate* (1970); and Richard Fried, *Men Against McCarthy* (1976). Fried provides the best analyses available of the impact of McCarthyism on the elections of 1950, 1952, and 1954, concluding that it was crucial in none of the three. Also informative on the politics of McCarthyism is a volume edited by Robert Griffith and Athan Theoharis, *The Specter: Original Essays on the Cold War and the Origins of McCarthyism* (1974). Two scholarly biographies of McCarthy have appeared in the past few years, each of which is balanced and well researched. Both Thomas Reeves's *The Life and Times of Joe McCarthy: A Biography* (1982) and David Oshinsky's *A Conspiracy So Immense: The World of Joe McCarthy* (1983) subscribe generally to the view that the McCarthy phenomenon reflected broad political forces, though Oshinsky, especially, underscores McCarthy's unique talents.

One of the myths that prevailed in early assessments of the Eisenhower years was that John Foster Dulles, rather than Eisenhower, controlled American foreign policy. The revisionist works of Parmet, Ambrose, and others have taken an opposite view, as have several recent works more specifically focused on foreign policy making. The most influential such study, even if very brief, is Robert Divine's *Eisenhower and the Cold War* (1981). Much more critical of Eisenhower's actions, but also portraying him as controlling policy, is Blanche Wiesen Cook *The Declassified Eisenhower: A Divided Legacy* (1981). Divine argues that Ike successfully moved toward meaningful accommodation with the Soviet Union, even while showing a willingness to consider the full range of options available to the United States in the Cold War. In contrast, Cook believes that Eisenhower wanted to avoid war, but committed the nation too extensively to wrongheaded (and evil) covert activities abroad. Burton Kaufman, in *Trade and Aid: Eisenhower's Foreign Economic Policy, 1953–1961* (1982), also portrays Eisenhower as a skillful and strong leader; though critical of specific policies, he is not nearly so harsh in his judgment as Cook.

Useful recently published works treating specific aspects of American foreign and defense policy in the Eisenhower years include Divine's *Blowing On the Wind: The Nuclear Test Ban Debate, 1945–1960* (1978); Donald Neff, *Warriors at Suez: Eisenhower Takes America into the Middle East* (1981); and

Richard E. Welch, Jr., *Responses to Revolution: The United States and the Cuban Revolution, 1959–1961* (1985). Of these three, only Welch is very critical of administration policies. Also informative on their respective subjects are Richard Aliano, *American Defense Policy from Eisenhower to Kennedy: The Politics of Changing Military Requirements, 1957–1961* (1975); Douglas Kinnard, *President Eisenhower and Strategy Management: A Study in Defense Politics* (1977); Roy Licklider, "The Missile Gap Controversy," *Political Science Quarterly* 85 (1970): 600–615; and Robert Divine, *Foreign Policy and U.S. Presidential Elections, 1952–1960* (1974), the companion to his volume on the three preceding elections.

The extensive CIA activities of the Eisenhower years are covered in a number of interesting studies. The best overall treatment is Stephen Ambrose, with Richard Immerman, *Ike's Spies: Eisenhower and the Espionage Establishment* (1981), which presents the pros and cons of the administration's covert activities in balanced fashion. Two books very critical of the successful CIA-inspired coup in Guatemala in 1954 are Richard Immerman, *The CIA in Guatemala: The Foreign Policy of Intervention* (1982), and Stephen Schlesinger and Stephen Kinzer, *Bitter Fruit: The Untold Story of the American Coup in Guatemala* (1982). Michael Beschloss's *Mayday: Eisenhower, Khrushchev and the U-2 Affair* (1986) attempts to resolve the riddles connected with the dramatic 1960 shootdown and subsequent events, holding both the Americans and the Soviets responsible for the debacle in May 1960.

Domestic issues in the 1950s have received less attention than foreign policy, and much less than similar matters in the Truman years. Gary Reichard, *The Reaffirmation of Republicanism: Eisenhower and the Eighty-third Congress* (1975), examines Eisenhower's policies and influence on congressional Republicans during the first two years of his presidency, arguing that he was both a fairly traditional Republican and a strong party leader. James Sundquist's *Politics and Policy: The Eisenhower, Kennedy, and Johnson Years* (1968) remains the only general study of Eisenhower's ongoing involvement in legislation over a range of domestic issue areas. Useful monographs are Alan McAdams, *Power and Politics in Labor Legislation* (1964), which traces development of the Landrum-Griffin Act; Aaron Wildavsky, *Dixon-Yates: A Study in Power Politics* (1962); Elmo Richardson, *Dams, Parks & Politics: Resource Development & Preservation in the Truman-Eisenhower Era* (1973); Mark Rose, *Interstate: Express Highway Politics, 1941-1956* (1979); and David Frier, *Conflict of Interest in the Eisenhower Administration* (1969).

Historians have been interested in the civil rights revolution in the Eisenhower era, and most have been critical of the president's reluctance to lead in this area. The best study of the subject is Robert Burk's *The Eisenhower Administration and Black Civil Rights* (1984), which depicts Eisenhower as committed to the rhetoric of racial equality, but limited in his actions by an antistatist philosophy. James Duram, *A Moderate Among Extremists: Dwight D. Eisenhower and the School Desegregation Crisis* (1981), takes much the same point of view. John Anderson's *Eisenhower, Brownell, and the Congress: The Tangled Origins of the Civil Rights Bill of 1956-1957* (1964) provides a detailed analysis of the major legislative struggle over civil rights during the Eisenhower years, while Numan Bartley, *The Rise of Massive Resistance: Race and Politics in the South During the 1950s* (1969), remains the most thorough work on the crisis over desegregation following the *Brown* decision. The middle chapters of Steven Lawson's *Black Ballots: Voting Rights in the South, 1944-1969* (1976) are instructive on both legislative developments and the political activities of the black community in the fifties.

Several memoirs provide insights into the Truman and Eisenhower administrations. Truman's two volumes—*Year of Decisions, 1945* (1953) and *Years of Trial and Hope, 1946-1952* (1956)—and Dean Acheson's *Present at the Creation: My Years in the State Department* (1969) are especially valuable sources on the early Cold War. Like Truman, Eisenhower produced two volumes, *Mandate for Change, 1953-1956* (1963) and *Waging Peace, 1956–1961* (1965). Also valuable are Sherman Adams, *Firsthand Report: The Story of the Eisenhower Administration* (1961), and Emmet Hughes, *The Ordeal of Power: A Political Memoir of the Eisenhower Years* (1963). Arthur Larson's *A Republican Looks at His Party* (1956) offers an extensive discussion of "Modern Republicanism" that reputedly met with Eisenhower's approval.

Biographies and autobiographies of congressional figures are often parochial and not very instructive about politics generally, but for the Truman and Eisenhower years, three biographies are exceptionally illuminating: Rowland Evans and Robert Novak, *Lyndon B. Johnson: The Exercise of Power* (1966); Herbert Parmet, *Jack: The Struggles of John F. Kennedy* (1980); and James Patterson, *Mr. Republican: A Biography of Robert A. Taft* (1972). Two autobiographies of interest are Albert Gore, *Let the Glory Out: My South and Its Politics* (1972), and Henry Cabot Lodge, *As It Was: An Inside View of Politics and Power in the '50s and '60s* (1976).

Several edited collections of personal papers also merit attention. The volume compiled by Arthur Vandenberg, Jr., *The Private Papers of Senator Vandenberg* (1952), is a revealing selection of the senator's letters on important subjects and events of the Truman years. Monte Poen has published a volume entitled *Strictly Personal and Confidential: The Letters Harry Truman Never Mailed* (1982), which documents Truman's extreme private reactions to important individuals and events. In addition, Robert Ferrell has edited three collections useful to those who cannot go to the Truman and Eisenhower Libraries to read the originals: *Off the Record: The Private Papers of Harry S. Truman* (1980); *The Eisenhower Diaries* (1981); and *The Diaries of James C. Hagerty: Eisenhower in Mid-Course, 1954–1955* (1983). Robert Griffith's *Ike's Letters to a Friend, 1941–1958* (1984) is a collection of the letters written by Eisenhower to one of his closest friends, Swede Hazlett, that present the president's private observations on a range of subjects.

On television as a political force in the Truman and Eisenhower years, useful material can be found in Robert Gilbert, *Television and Presidential Politics* (1972), and the memoirs of CBS executive Fred Friendly, *Due to Circumstances Beyond Our Control . . .* (1968).

Four insightful contemporary works on voter behavior in the period are Samuel Lubell, *The Future of American Politics* (1952; revised in 1965), which is especially good on the years through 1952; *Revolt of the Moderates* (1956), also by Lubell; Louis Harris, *Is There a Republican Majority? Political Trends, 1952–1956* (1954); and a much more methodical study by Survey Research Center scholars Angus Campbell, Philip Converse, Warren Miller, and Donald Stokes, *The American Voter* (1960). Probably the most valuable recent work on voting trends in the Truman and Eisenhower years is Everett Ladd, Jr., with Charles Hadley, *Transformations in the American Party System: Political Coalitions from the New Deal to the 1970s* (rev. ed., 1978). Still a standard on the 1960 election is Philip Converse, et al., "Stability and Change in 1960: A Reinstating Election," *American Political Science Review* 55 (1961): 269–280.

INDEX

reorganization (1958), 141
  spending, 92, 95, 155
demobilization, 3–4
Democratic Advisory Committee
  (DAC), 133, 135–136, 138, 140
desegregation:
  See civil rights
Dewey, Thomas E., 14, 20
  and election of 1948, 35, 37–39,
  41, 42–43
Dien Bien Phu, 94
Dirksen, Everett, 99, 101, 107, 157
Divine, Robert, 111, 113, 145, 153
Dixiecrats:
  See Southern Democrats, States'
  Rights Democrats (1948)
Dixon, Edgar, 119
Dixon-Yates scandal, 119
Donovan, Robert, 38, 54–55, 60,
  70–71
Douglas, Helen Gahagan, 65
Douglas, Paul, 44, 106, 133
Douglas, William O., 34
Duff, James, 79
Dulles, Allen, 114
Dulles, John Foster, 14, 91, 93, 94,
  95, 97, 99, 110, 112, 114, 124,
  128–129, 148, 171
Duram, James, 135, 137

Eastland, James, 35, 36, 90, 117,
  133, 136
economy
  See also employment; inflation;
  labor-management relations;
  national debt; price controls;
  taxes
  and elections, 126–127, 146, 147,
  162
Eden, Sir Anthony, 128
education
  See also National Defense
  Education Act; Powell
  Amendment
  federal aid to, 39, 49, 73, 116
Eisenhower, Dwight D., 34, 66, 67,
  165, 166, 167
  and Bricker Amendment, 96–98
  and CIA, 139, 149, 152–153

and Castro, 152–153
and civil rights, 88–89, 117, 132–
  137, 157, 169
and Cold War, 97, 99, 110, 112–
  113, 120, 129, 136, 139, 145,
  149–151
and Congress, 109–110, 113
and election of 1952, 78–83
and elections of 1954, 105
and election of 1956, 121–127,
  130
and election of 1960, 159, 162,
  164
health of, 120, 122, 129–130, 142
and Korean War, 91
and McCarthyism, 98, 100–101,
  107–108
and missiles, 139–143
presidency assessed, 168–172
as president, 84–166
and Suez crisis, 124–125, 127–128
and U-2 crisis, 150–151
Eisenhower, Mamie, 80
Eisenhower, Milton, 89, 166
Eisenhower Doctrine, 128, 144
  See also Middle East Resolution
Eisenhower Republicanism, 86, 87,
  131, 132, 171
elections
  of 1944, 1–2, 14, 31
  of 1946, 16–19, 28
  of 1948, 26, 27, 32–45
  of 1950, 64–65
  of 1952, 74, 75, 77–84, 85, 97, 98
  of 1954, 104–106, 114
  of 1956, 120–127
  of 1958, 146–147
  of 1960, 153–154, 158–166, 167
Elsey, George, 65
Employee Loyalty Program, 24, 57–
  58
  See also Loyalty Review Board
employment, 4, 6–7, 106
  assistance, 72
Employment Act of 1946, 6–7, 47
Ervin, Sam, 104
European Recovery Program (ERP):
  See Marshall Plan
Evans, Rowland, 48, 133

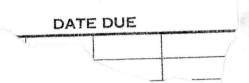
Politics as Usual: The Age of Truman and Eisenhower was copyedited by Anita Samen. Production editor was Brad Barrett. The text was proofread by Martha Kreger. The book was typeset by Impressions, Inc., and printed and bound by Lithocolor Press, Inc.

Cover and book design by Roger Eggers.